J

1495

W9-BHZ-133

THE GREEN GARDEN

This book is for Larry, who loved trees.

· GARDENING · BY · DESIGN ·

THE GREEN GARDEN

THE ART OF FOLIAGE PLANTING

· LYS · DE · BRAY ·

Salem House Publishers
Topsfield, Massachusetts

ACKNOWLEDGEMENTS

All the photographs were taken by Bob Challinor.

The Publishers are grateful to the owners of the following gardens for granting permission to have their gardens photographed: Burford House Gardens, Shropshire, (pp. 11, 14) ; Savill Gardens, nr. Windsor (pp. 15 & 18); Hidcote Manor Gardens, Gloucestershire (pp. 19, 22 & 30); Cotswold Farm, Gloucestershire (p. 34); Bodnant Gardens, Gwynedd (pp. 42, 43 & 51); Spinners, Hampshire (p. 54). Hidcote Manor Garden is a National Trust Garden; Burford House Garden, Cotswold Farm and Spinners are National Gardens Scheme gardens.

All the line drawings are by Lys de Bray. The publishers are grateful to the author for granting permission to reproduce the botanical drawings.

© Ward Lock Limited 1988

First published in the United States by Salem House Publishers, 1988, 462 Boston Street, Topsfield, Massachusetts, 01983.

Library of Congress Cataloging in Publication Data:

De Bray, Lys.
The green garden.

(Gardening by design)
1. Foliage plants. 2. Landscape gardening.
I. Title. II. Series.
SB431.D4 1988   715   88-3061
ISBN 0-88162-331-8

Printed and bound by Graficromo s.a., Cordoba, Spain

CONTENTS

PREFACE

All gardeners will have noticed that it is difficult, if not impossible, to keep a garden looking good throughout the year. The flowering plants do not always do as well as expected for climatic or other reasons and some need almost constant attention. Then there are the colour-gaps when the whole garden looks dispirited and untidy half-way through the season.

This book suggests how whole gardens – or specific areas in larger gardens – can be planned and planted for foliage interest. There are lists of all kinds of trees, shrubs, ferns, grasses and waterside plants to help you in your choice. All of these have a much longer season of interest than the average border plant, many are evergreen, and many, of course, have flowers which can be part of the garden plan; since they are not of paramount importance, they will not be missed when they are over. Foliage plants can be used to soften or hide the sharp edges of unfortunate architecture, they complement good modern design, and they blend naturally with older, more gracious building styles. Foliage plants are not just green, they can be chosen in colours of grey, white, silver, black, red, crimson, purple, bronze, blue or quite wonderful variegations, with autumnal colouration often adding a second season of interest. Once established, gardens planted with foliage plants are very restful because there is less actual gardening to do and, aesthetically, such gardens are places of tranquillity and harmony.

L. de B.

1

WHAT KIND OF GARDENER?

This is a question which must be answered honestly before you read any further. To help with this soul search I have listed some categories below. You may slot into one, or several; they are merely a helpful peg on which to hang your gardener's hat.

FLOWER-ARRANGER

Flower-arrangers are 'consumer' gardeners, needing to grow vast quantities of interesting foliage plants of all kinds and for all seasons. This kind of gardener will collect plants voraciously and often needs several or even large drifts of single species, because constant 'pruning' means that the plants cannot regenerate quickly enough. Therefore, in a flower-arranger's garden you will find disproportionately large groups of such stalwarts as alchemilla and artemisia, ballota and bergenia and so on, but hopefully they will be planted to complement one another. Almost all the plants in Chapter 7 can be used for arrangements.

THE AESTHETE

The aesthete need not have a large garden, but what there is needs to be as perfect as possible from all view-points. This kind of gardener will use each season to improve on the planting harmonies of the preceding year, and will usually be cautiously selective, choosing plants for shape, colour, texture and form as well as interest.

THE COLLECTOR

The collector's garden may be small, but it can be very interesting to its owner and like-minded friends. In such a garden might be found a collection of ivies (*Hedera*), ferns, dwarf conifers chosen for colour and contrast of form, graceful grasses and sedges, or the round crownlike shapes of sempervivum.

THE BUSY GARDENER

Many people would like to have gardens to be proud of, but for economical reasons may not have very much time in which to make them a source of pride and admiration. Many of the plants listed in Chapter 7 will help the image and improve the value of the property; they will remain neat for very long periods with little attention. The choice of plants is more limited here, but is nevertheless pleasing.

[Text continues on p. 12

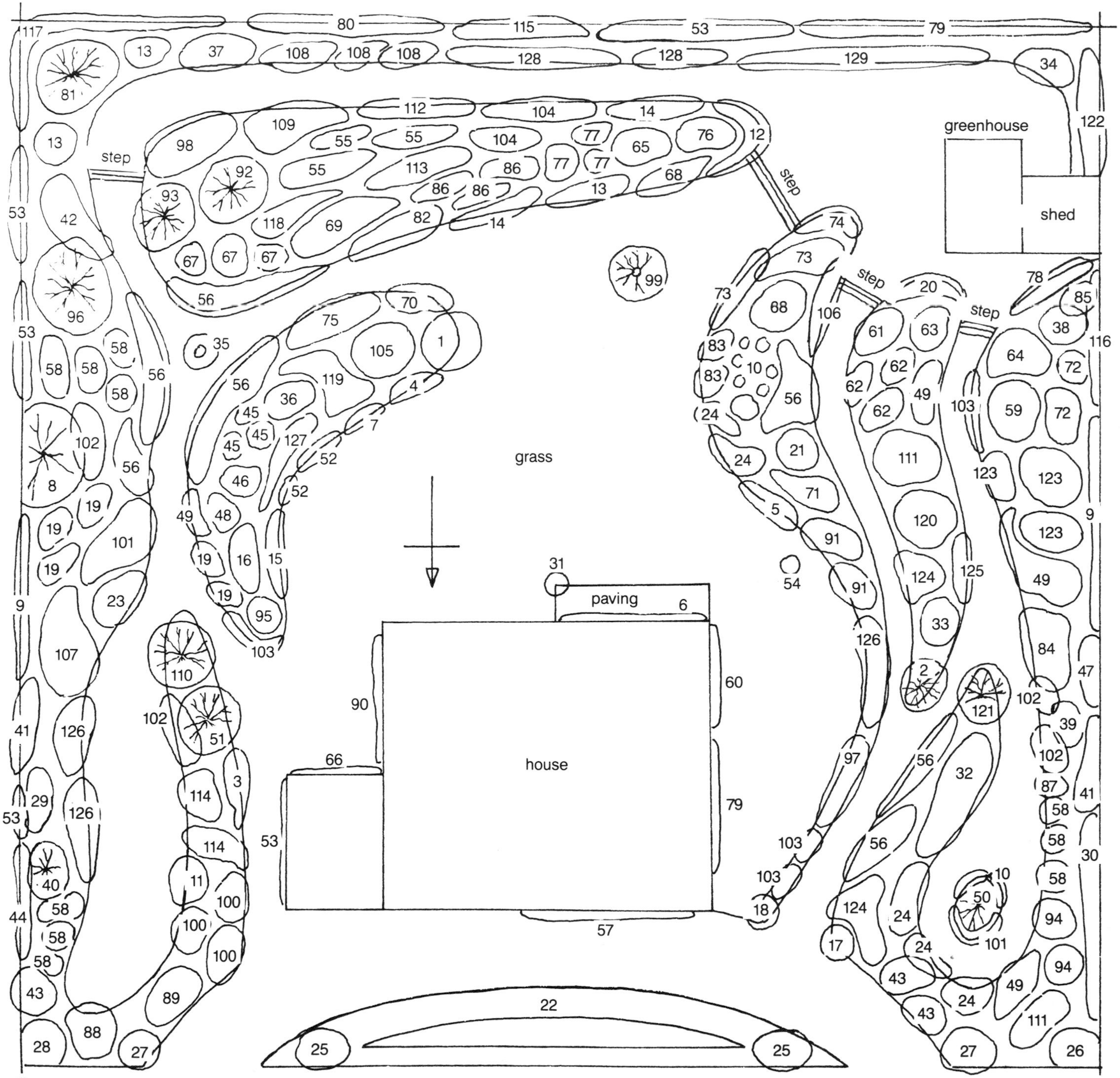

117
80
115
53
79

13
37
108
108
108
128
128
129
34

81

112
104
14
122

13
98
109
55
55
104
77
76
12
greenhouse

step
92
55
113
86
77
77
65
68
step

93
86
86
13
74

42
118
69
82
73
shed

67
67
67
14
73
step
20
78

96
56
73
68
106
step
85

70
83
61
63
38

53
75
35
105
1
83
10
62
64
72
116

56
119
4
24
62
49
103
59
72

58
36
7
56
21
111
123

58
58
56
45
127
24
71
120
123

58
45
45
52
5
91
124
125
49

56
46
52
91
9

102
49
48
grass
54
126

8
19
16
15
33
84

19
19
101
23
31
2
102

19
95
paving
6
121
39

103
110
60
102

107
102
90
97
56
32
87
41

51
house
79
58
30

41
126
3
53
103
56

29
114
103
124
94

53
126
18
17
24
50

40
114
57
94

58
11
100
22
43
24
101

44
58
100
25
25
43
24
49

58
100
27
26

43

28
89

88
27

8

Fig. 1. The Flower-Arranger's Garden

Large quantities of interesting foliage are of more use to flower-arrangers than flowers, curiously enough. Flowers can be bought, but a continuous supply of foliage would be very expensive. This plan has been designed for a garden that is aesthetically pleasing and restful to look at, as well as being useful year-round. There are many places where small plants (not shown or listed because of the scale of the drawing) can be introduced.

1. Cotinus coggygria 'Royal Purple'
2. Acer pseudoplatanus 'Leopoldii'
3. Acanthus mollis or Acanthus spinosus
4. Cornus controversa
5. Acer palmatum 'Atropurpureum'
6. Actinidia kolomikta
7. Aegopodium
8. Ailanthus altissima
9. Akebia quinata
10. Angelica archangelica
11. Aralia elata
12. Lavandulas
13. Taxus baccata
14. Ligustrum
15. Artemisia ludoviciana
16. Berberis thunbergii 'Atropurpurea'
17. Arundinaria nitida
18. Arundinaria viridistriata
19. Aucubas
20. Ballota pseudodictamnus
21. Buddleia alternifolia
22. Formal planting, heathers if acid soil
23. Cercidiphyllum japonicum
24. Bergenia
25. Chamaecyparis lawsoniana 'Lutea'
26. Chamaecyparis lawsoniana 'Pembury Blue'
27. Chamaecyparis pisifera 'Boulevard'
28. Chamaecyparis pisifera 'Squarrosa'
29. Choisya ternata
30. Clematis armandii
31. Cordyline or Trachycarpus
32. Cornus alba 'Elegantissima'
33. Corylus maxima 'Purpurea'
34. Cotoneaster
35. Statue, with Cyclamen vars. around the base
36. Cynara scolymus
37. Cytisus battandieri
38. Elaeagnus commutata
39. Elaeagnus pungens 'Maculata'
40. Eucalyptus gunnii
41. Euonymus 'Silver Queen'
42. Euonymus 'Emerald 'n Gold'
43. Fatsias
44. Fatshedera
45. Foeniculum vulgare 'Purpureum'
46. Fuchsia magellanica 'Gracilis variegata'
47. Garrya elliptica
48. Genista aetnensis
49. Geranium macrorrhizum
50. Ginkgo biloba
51. Gleditschia triacanthos 'Sunburst'
52. Ajugas
53. Hederas
54. Statue or urn on plinth with Helichrysum petiolatum
55. Hippophae rhamnoides
56. Hostas
57. Hydrangea petiolaris
58. Ilex
59. Itea ilicifolia
60. Jasminum officinale 'Aurea'
61. Juniperus communis 'Hornibrookii'
62. Juniperus communis 'Grey Owl'
63. Koelreuteria paniculata
64. Ligustrum ovalifolium 'Aureomarginatum'
65. Ligustrum vulgare 'Aureum'
66. Lonicera japonica 'Aureoreticulata'
67. Lonicera nitida
68. Lonicera nitida 'Baggesen's Gold'
69. Lunaria biennis
70. Lychnis coronaria
71. Macleaya cordata
72. Mahonias
73. Melianthus major
74. Miscanthus vars.
75. Nepeta
76. Olearia macrodonta
77. Onopordon acanthium
78. Origanum vulgare 'Aureum'
79. Parthenocissus henryana
80. Parthenocissus quinquefolia
81. Paulownia tomentosa
82. Peltiphyllum peltatum
83. Phalaris arundinacea 'Picta'
84. Philadelphus coronaria 'Aurea'
85. Phlomis fruticosa
86. Phormiums
87. Tolmeia
88. Weigela florida 'Variegata'
89. Physocarpus opulifolius 'Lutea'
90. Pileostegia viburnoides
91. Pittosporum tenuifolium
92. Populus alba
93. Prunus cerasifera 'Atropurpurea'
94. Prunus laurocerasus
95. Pyrus salicifolia 'Pendula'
96. Quercus coccinea 'Splendens'
97. Rheum palmatum 'Rubrum'
98. Rhus typhina
99. Robinia pseudoacacia 'Frisia'
100. Rosa rubrifolia
101. Rubus tricolor
102. Ruscus aculeatus
103. Ruta
104. Salvias (shrubby)
105. Sambucus racemosa 'Plumosa Aurea'
106. Santolina chamaecyparissus
107. Sasa palmata
108. Sedums
109. Senecio greyi
110. Sorbus aria
111. Spartium junceum
112. Stachys lanata
113. Tamarix
114. Viburnum davidii
115. Humulus lupulus 'Aurea'
116. Vitis coignetiae
117. Vitis vinifera 'Purpurea'
118. Zea
119. Ricinus
120. Thuja occidentalis 'Rheingold'
121. Acer 'Leopoldii'
122. Hedera 'Buttercup'
123. Ferns
124. Lamiastrum galeobdolon
125. Mitella breweri
126. Epimediums
127. Curtonus
128. Eryngiums
129. Dianthus vars.

In a larger garden conifers provide living sculptures in a variety of textures and tones.

A harmony of shape and colour here in dry semi-shade beneath a tree, *Smilacina racemosa*, Pulmonarias and the obliging *Senecio greyi*.

THE SLOTH

Most of us are lazy at heart. There are a number of very useful plants which can be relied on for loyalty to this kind of gardener whose main gardening tool need only be pruning shears. Grass may not be a good idea in this garden as it can wear a reproachful look after about three weeks.

THE OWNER OF A FORMAL GARDEN

Where plants are used to clothe or decorate masonry, paving, statuary, architectural features or other formal areas, these plants are, as it were, extra embroidery in a design and should, if possible, be beautiful or interesting in all seasons, though the choice is more limited here for this reason.

THE ELDERLY, INFIRM OR DISABLED GARDENER

With very little work after the initial effort of planting, the elderly and disabled can have a delightful and satisfactory garden. At times of real incapacity neighbours or relatives who are not even gardeners can do the minimal tasks necessary to keep this kind of gardener in good heart until he or she is well again.

THE ABSENTEE GARDENER

This gardener needs to have a presentable and attractive garden with the minimum of weekend attention. Grass is not a good idea here either, because someone has to cut it, so paving or gravel is almost essential.

Hedera helix

2

WHAT KIND OF GARDEN?

The term 'garden' covers everything from the smallest town basement to the largest of apparently unmanageable acres, and includes sections of gardens otherwise devoted to flowers, fruit and vegetables. It should be remembered that a foliage garden, once planned, planted and growing well is the most tranquil of places to be because it does not change as much as the conventional border, which can vary from comparative nudity in mid-winter through to the lush burgeonings of summer glory, the brilliance of autumnal colour and so back to dormancy and decay before the cycle begins again. This is a 'normal' garden.

THE TOWN GARDEN

At one end of the garden scale there are small town plots, of varying shapes and aspects (the latter should always be taken into account). However difficult the conditions, even the darkest basement corner can be changed into a place of interest and beauty, and there are plenty of excellent plants which are quite happy in these conditions.

THE DIFFICULT POSITION

This type of garden may be hot and dry, or cold, or sited on a windy slope (or all of these) but, never fear,

there are plants to suit, though many may be flowering shrubs whose colours may interfere with your careful plan. Picking the flowers for vases indoors will solve this minor problem. Gardens in frost pockets should be sensibly planted with really hardy plants, so turn your back (with resolution) on the semi-tender treasures in the catalogues whose expensive replacements have died of frost-bite for the third successive winter.

Seasonal dormancy is acceptable to the gardener and essential to many plants; this period of quiescence is very useful, as during this time plants can be moved and generally rearranged to improve the appearance of the garden.

DAMP GARDENS

Permanently damp gardens are not a problem so long as plants are chosen that thrive in these conditions. In very cold winters the frost may bite very deep into the ground, so this should be remembered when choosing your plants.

If Mediterranean-type plants are passionately desired (and there is sun to match) then plan raised beds with plenty of drainage; this will lift the rosemaries, the lavenders and all the cliff-dwellers up from the ground and give them a dryer habitat, though dwarf-growing varieties should be chosen or they may tower above you as they do in the real maquis.

[Text continues on p. 17

In a sheltered sunny glade the handsome shapes of *Rodgersia tabularis* make a substantial contrast in shape to the delicacy of bamboo beyond.

Here is grandeur, achieved gradually over a period of time; the cascading waterfall of *Salix babylonica* making a delicately beautiful contrast to conifers, berberis, ligustrum and mahonia.

Fig 2.   The Garden for the Elderly, Infirm or Disabled

This garden is relatively easy to maintain, with no
rampant climbers or trees to worry about. (The
vegetable plot seemed to be essential; see also p. 12.)

1. Dianthus or Cerastium or Alchemilla
2. Lavandula (dwarf vars.)
3. Pileostegia
4. Choisya ternata
5. Origanum vulgare 'Aureum'
6. Ajuga
7. Salvia 'Purpurascens'
8. Ballota
9. Taxus
10. Bergenia or Alchemilla
11. Tamarix
12. Euonymus 'Silver Queen'
13. Chamaecyparis pisifera 'Boulevard'
14. Lavandula or Artemisia ludoviciana
15. Rosa rubrifolia
16. Hedera 'Buttercup'
17. Bergenia
18. Sambucus racemosa 'Plumosa Aurea'
19. Weigela florida 'Foliis Purpureis'
20. Griselinia
21. Hedera
22. Cotinus coggygria
23. Lysimachia nummularia 'Aurea'
24. Phalaris arundinacea 'Picta' (plant in old
     buckets)
25. Cornus alba 'Elegantissima'
26. Saxifraga × urbium
27. Fastigiate conifer
28. Viburnum davidii (male and female)
29. Ferns
30. Aucuba
31. Lamiastrum galeobdolon
32. Juniperus communis 'Hornibrookii'
33. Bergenias or Alchemilla
34. Elaeagnus pungens 'Maculata'

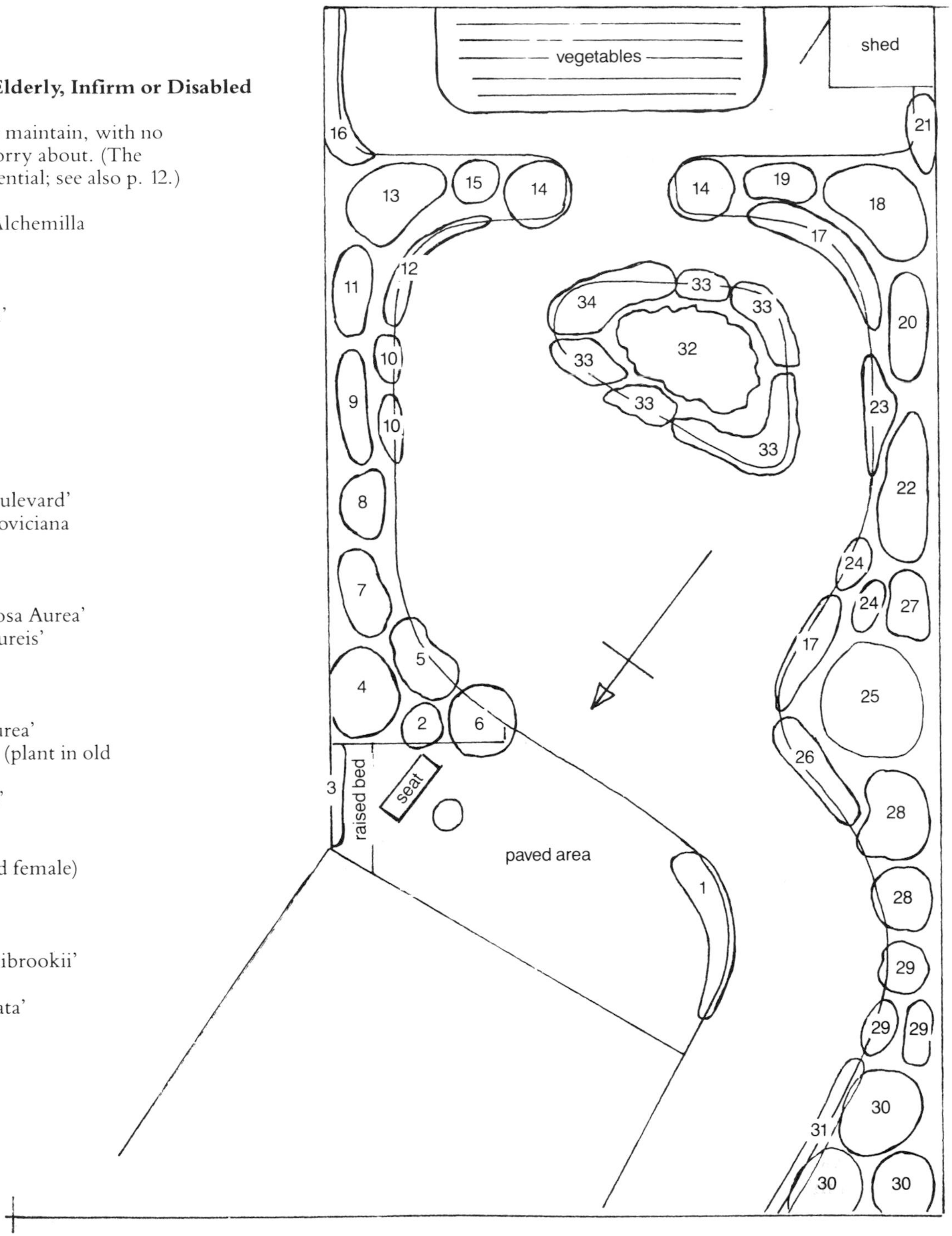

THE LARGE GARDEN

The almost-too-large-to-cope-with garden becomes manageable with foliage plants, large areas of grass and good groups of shrubs and trees, though these will take time to mature. In this case it is best to draw a plan, having first decided how much (or how little) gardening you want to undertake throughout the year.

THE NEW GARDEN

Starting a garden from scratch can be, at one and the same time, an exciting challenge, a hoped-for dream or a frightening and dispiriting spectacle after the builders have departed, taking your topsoil with them. This last (and the builders) are not going to return, so make the best of it and import as many truck-loads of good soil as you can afford, making sure that it matches the pH value of the soil in your area.

THE NEGLECTED GARDEN

An overgrown garden is slightly more comforting, and may even have some unexpected treasures which will give your 'new' garden instant maturity, even though the treasures may be in the wrong place. For the time being it really is best, in this case, to see a whole year round; you may feel you are wasting time but this can be used to good effect by visiting nurseries and other gardens, learning where the best and the worst parts of the garden are, making plans on paper and ordering shrubs, plants, trees and climbers that will transform your untidy Eden. The transformation scene can begin in early autumn, though you are quite likely to be still at it at Easter. Winter is always the best time for real gardening, in any case, paying handsome dividends in the following summer for your effort.

THE SUBURBAN STRIP

These long, thin gardens are almost the hardest situation for this kind of gardening, because it is not always easy to garden in blinkers, which is necessary in order not to be distracted by the gardens on each side. Wherever possible, try to erect sturdy fencing of some kind unless hedges already exist. In some cases, the constitution of the hedge may not be to your liking but almost any hedge is better than none at all, and a stout laurel hedge can be a decided asset. Privet, if leggy and gappy at the bottom should be replaced (along with its old and exhausted soil) before you start on your garden proper, as pulling out an old and neglected hedge at a later date can cause all kinds of accidental damage. Within the hedged or fenced rectangle you can plan an interesting collection of plants, in privacy, and in time you may well convert your neighbours to an interest in the subtleties and fascination of foliage.

THE POCKET HANDKERCHIEF

The very small garden is hard to plant because the precious inches have to be utilized to the best advantage. Choose small neat plants, even tiny ones where these are to be viewed the most (through glass patio doors, for example) and try to keep everything in scale. If choosing phormiums, choose dwarf varieties; if conifers, look for the description 'slow growing' on the label. There will be three planting sites in a modern 'development' garden – the ground itself, a wall or a fence, and your tubs, troughs or pots which can be selected in a range of different heights. If space permits, a raised bed can be made in one or two corners, thus providing three more growing areas – the flat top of the bed, the wall behind it, and the front wall of the raised bed itself which can have planting holes incorporated at the time of construction.

The glaucous blue of hostas is a beautiful foil to the finely dissected green foliage of the acer.

Ferns have a charming habit of sowing themselves into the most appropriate places, as here with the old stone statue.

3

PLANT ASSOCIATIONS

Setting out a foliage garden in mid-winter requires three-dimensional thinking. At all times, one must remember the shape, the height and the ultimate spread of the plant – for example, a single alchemilla left to itself is a thing of beauty, with a round central corona of pleated leaves surrounded by an even petticoat-frill of tiny lime green flowers. The whole thing measures about 1.2 m (4 ft) from wing-tip to wing-tip and it is not often that there is such space available, nor is it really practical to garden in this way, as the alchemilla is dormant in winter, grows to flowering maturity in mid-summer and will then need to be tidied up after a month or so. For real satisfaction in gardening, try to plant sharp, spiky-leaved things such as iris and neat, rounded mounding plants such as geraniums together which makes both shapes satisfying because of the extreme contrast. Plant amorphous, cloudy shapes like fennel as a background to firmer, more solid plants that have a good clear outline: the leaves of arum lilies, or hostas, or the annual castor-oil plant, *Ricinus communis*, which comes in green or crimson-bronze.

Feathery-leaved plants such as the astilbes, thalictrums and aruncus should not be set next to each other or to similar plants because the beauty of their dissected foliage will be lost. These need as companions either upright sword-leaved plants such as curtonus, iris or canna, or foliage with graceful curves such as montbretia, crocosmia or hemerocallis, while hostas are good with all of these.

Some taller plants are beautiful at the top but their legs need to be concealed, and this can be done by setting shorter plants such as geraniums, *Heuchera* 'Palace Purple', a rounded shrub such as dorycnium or one of the artemisias in front, though not too close or the tall chap will lose out on the rainfall.

Many of the silver- or grey-leaved plants have exceedingly beautiful foliage, which is often finely dissected, as in *Artemisia* 'Lambrook Silver', *Artemisia schmidtiana* 'Nana' and the little feathers of *Tanacetum densum amani*. To look their best, these need plants of different or toning colours and shapes close by. *Artemisia* 'Lambrook Silver', for example, looks well with the striking contrast of purple orache, *Atriplex hortensis* 'Purpurea', or if something more subtle is desired, try the exquisite foliage plant *Melianthus major* (this has bare stems after the first year which generally need a little concealment). The classical leaves of *Acanthus mollis* are exceedingly handsome (and the plant will not flower if grown in semi-shade) and a group may be set off by a small-leaved ground covering plant such as the yellow-leaved creeping Jenny, *Lysimachia nummularia* 'Aurea' or a mat of *Helxine soleirolii*. Other contrasts for silver-leaved plants are the various ajugas, particularly *A. metallica*, yellow marjoram (*Origanum vulgare* 'Aureum'), the annual *Kochia scoparia* or the easy-going ice plant, *Sedum spectabile* whose pale green leaves are beautiful from early spring onwards. The flower buds of this remain green until late summer, and the flower heads may be removed when they begin to glow pink. Interplant groups of similar silver- or grey-leaved things with plants of a different foliage colour and texture or the delicate, frosty charm of the former will not have so much impact.

[Text continues on p. 24

Fig. 3.   The Formal Garden

This apparently simple design and planting scheme is very elegant – it is also very labour-saving. The statues should all be different. (See also p. 12.)

1. Cotoneaster
2. Taxus baccata
3. Coleus or Bergenia or Hedera
4. Canna or Curtonus or Macleaya or Cynara
5. Statues or urns with Helichrysum petiolatum

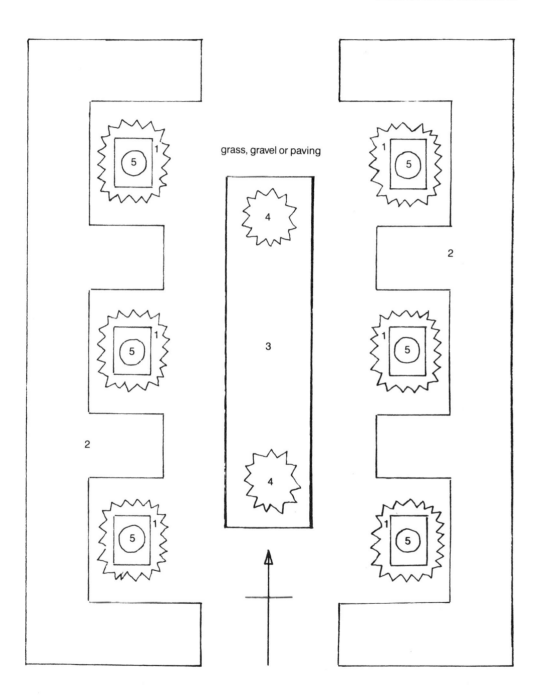

This path has textural interest on either side, with epimedium, ferns, grasses, hostas and ricinus in the background.

The gracefully curving leaves of hemerocallis set off the large, bold foliage of *Rheum palmatum*, with the fern *Matteuccia struthiopteris* behind.

If space permits, think big. Plant a blue gum, *Eucalyptus gunnii*, near a plum-purple *Prunus cerasifera* 'Atropurpurea' (the variety 'Nigra' has even darker leaves). Alternatively, you could plant the smoke bush, *Cotinus coggygria*, either the species, or named varieties of even finer performance, such as *C.c.* 'Foliis Purpureis' or *C.c.* 'Royal Purple'. Another dark-leaved shrub (really a tree, but it can be kept pruned down to shrub-size for a considerable time) is the copper beech, *Fagus sylvatica* 'Purpurea', (more properly called *F.s.* 'Riversii', syn. 'Rivers' Purple') which is the darkest of all. Nearby you could set the yellow-leaved *Physocarpus opulifolius* 'Luteus' which can be kept pruned down to manageability, or, alternatively, the golden elder, *Sambucus racemosa plumosa* 'Aurea' could be used, or the yellow weigela, *Weigela* 'Looymansii Aurea'. To add even further interest, set a New Zealand flax, *Phormium tenax* in front of the physocarpus, and when the new branches of lime-yellow leaves form in the spring, they will arch up and trail down through the stiff fans of the phormium leaves. This is quite beautiful in my garden.

Other, more miniature, contrasts can be arranged at the edges of paths or in the smallest of small gardens. I have *Acaena microphylla* in a sunny pocket of soil near the pond. This has mats of exquisite tiny bronze-green leaves with whitish flower globes (not colourful, but interesting: these are followed later by hookless crimson burs). The acaena has the dark green grassy leaves of *Armeria maritima* nearby for contrast of form and shape, and the unlikely foliage of chives, *Allium schoenoprasum*, adds more interest, particularly as one is supposed to pick the flowers off in any case. The silver-edged foliage of *Alchemilla alpina* and the Alice-through-the-looking-glass crowns of sempervivums complete this pleasing corner, while above all is an airy, small-leaved shrub, *Corokia cotoneaster*, often called the 'wire-netting bush' because its branches resemble a bundle of wire-netting in colour and appearance. A dwarf-growing conifer could be used here instead, if more solidity is preferred.

The grass family is very versatile and all of them are beautiful. The small blue-green tufts of *Festuca glauca* may be just what is needed to complete an edging scheme, which might be further improved by the pink-purple rosettes of *Ajuga reptans* 'Burgundy Glow' or *A.r. metallica*.

Where there is space for the graceful foliage of larger grasses, then try one of the varieties of *Miscanthus sinensis*, of which *M.s.* 'Zebrinus' is one of the best, with yellow-striped leaves and no flowering plumes to speak of. This plant is tall, to 2.1 m (7 ft) sometimes, so perhaps the graceful *Achnatherum calamagrostis* (often found, wrongly, in the catalogues as *Stipa calamagrostis*) could be considered instead, as it grows only to 90 cm (3 ft) with soft violet plumes that fade to a beautiful silvery beige. This and other grasses look their best when grown with companions of such different shapes and colours as *Griselinia littoralis*, with its pleasant apple-green leaves, the soft greyness of *Ballota pseudodictamnus*, or the handsome jade-green sculptural leaves of *Macleaya cordata* which has the most beautiful foliage in the garden. Nearby you could plant a bronze fennel, *Foeniculum vulgare* 'Purpureum', with a touch of variegation at its feet in the shape of the well-mannered ground elder, *Aegopodium podagraria* 'Variegata', useful in any conditions except shade. The smart green and white stripes of gardener's garters, *Phalaris arundinacea* 'Picta' echo this theme and are very striking in a border, though its colonizing propensities should be remembered (and curbed by being planted in an old bucket). To set it off, the solid leaves of bergenia can be grown alongside, with the acid light yellow-green of the shuttlecock fern *Matteuccia struthiopteris*, which will grow quite well in an ordinary border. It is a continuing and fascinating form of gardening to grow plants for their foliage and form, making for endless interest and experiment because there is no real hurry – there is a whole season ahead, unlike the often too-short burst of glory of flowering plants and shrubs. The flowers of some of the plants named are not conspicuous, and can be left, though the purist foliage gardener may like to remove them.

4

ESSENTIAL EVERGREENS

The main components of this kind of garden are the permanent structure-plants, which should be evergreen for two reasons – the first being to avoid winter bareness and the second because they are labour-saving. (Also, as conservationists will know, birds prefer gardens with plenty of evergreen cover in winter.) The choice of plants will depend on the space available, the type of soil and general aspect of the garden or this part of a larger garden. To a lesser degree, availability is also important, as some very interesting plants are not common and may take a while to find, and in a small garden where space matters – or, rather, the lack of it, it is best to see what something unusual really looks like, rather than succumbing to a glowing description in a catalogue, waiting for delivery and then enduring several seasons of sometimes disappointing performance.

To start with, one of the obvious stalwarts – yew, *Taxus baccata*. The common kind grows surprisingly quickly – my self-sown seedling has achieved an inconvenient and rapid growth of some 3.6 m (12 ft) in about eleven years. But it does act as a foil to the rose 'Dorothy Perkins' and two beautiful vines, so it will have to stay where it is (in addition, it is the end-post of my washing line). Yew comes in a variety of green types, such as the elegant fastigiate (narrowly columnar) *T.b.* 'Fastigiata' or gold 'Fastigiata Aureomarginata'. In addition there are variegated-leaved types, one being *T.b.* 'Variegata' (or 'Argentea') (leaves becoming edged with grey-white) or *T.b.* 'Adpressa Variegata' (syn. 'Adpressa Aurea') whose leaves unfold old-gold and fade to a lighter colour as the season advances. Yew makes the best hedge or background possible and does well on both chalk or acid soils.

Holly, *Ilex* spp., makes another excellent background when the ordinary dark green-leaved *Ilex aquifolium* is chosen. A hedge grows quickly, but must (as with all hedging shrubs) be kept clipped from the first to promote thick bushy growth at the base. Never be tempted to let tall-growing hedging plants grow as fast as they would like to, or you will have a lacy smoke-screen rather than a solid green wall. There are a tremendous number of varieties with yellow, cream or white variegated leaves in all permutations from almost smooth to downright vicious when it comes to prickles, but this is to be expected and is most interesting when they are grown in a collection, as at Kew. In addition, where male and female plants are present, there will be berries in many shades of red, yellow or amber.

Box, *Buxus sempervirens*, is generally used as low internal hedging or for topiary work, and its neat leaves, compact habit and longevity make it perfect for this. The leaves are aromatic when clipped, making this task a pleasure. The shiny-sticky foliage of escallonia makes a good hedge or screen in coastal gardens, though it can be tender in cold inland areas. It can be kept neat with clipping, but is vigorous and needs space and sun. Pyracantha is another shrub which needs space and sun to do well; it is an amazingly good-natured plant, seeming not to mind when or how much it is pruned. It is generally grown for the berries which provide plenty of food for the birds in hard winters.

[Text continues on p. 29

The formality of clipped yew makes an enduring background for the light green arching foliage of hemerocallis and the dissected leaves of the tree peony.

There is a long season of interest in this border, with the handsome dark foliage of the hellebore seen against its background of light green willow leaves.

27

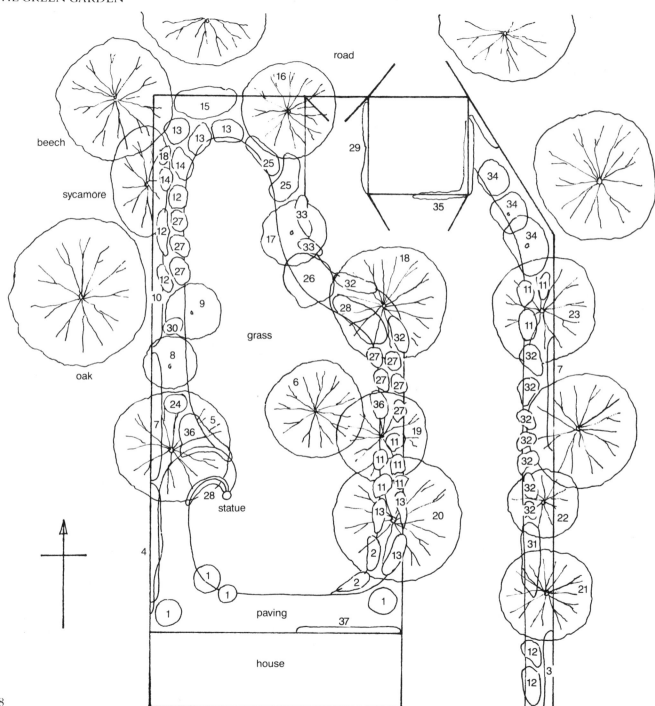

road

beech

sycamore

oak

grass

statue

paving

37

house

Fig. 4. The Shaded Garden

Shade is wonderful on a hot day and in hot climates. Sometimes it is almost unavoidable, owing to the trees in neighbouring gardens and street planting. Many plants are quite happy in this environment.

1. Colcus
2. Mitella breweri
3. Parthenocissus henryana
4. Hydrangea petiolaris
5. Taxodium distichum
6. Quercus coccinea
7. Hedera
8. Cercidiphyllum japonicum
9. Golden conifer
10. × Fatshedera lizei
11. Ruscus aculeatus
12. Ruta
13. Bergenia
14. Milium effusum 'Aureum'
15. Cornus alba 'Elegantissima'
16. Salix babylonica
17. Bamboo
18. Eucalyptus gunnii
19. Robinia pseudoacacia 'Frisia'
20. Prunus cerasifera 'Pissardii'
21. Ilex (male) variegated
22. Ilex (female) green
23. Fagus sylvatica 'Riversii'
24. Galium odoratum
25. Geranium macrorrhizum
26. Weigela florida 'Variegata'
27. Hostas
28. Cyclamen
29. Akebia quinata
30. Ruta
31. Lamiastrum galeobdolon
32. Alchemilla mollis
33. Saxifraga × urbium
34. Viburnum davidii (male and female)
35. Clematis armandii
36. Ferns
37. Garrya elliptica

The common privet, *Ligustrum vulgare*, does make a quick-growing hedge but is better not planted unless the conditions are so dreadful that all other plant material has perished. In this case one can welcome privet, but plant *L.v.* 'Aureus', the gold-leaved kind, which is not quite as vigorous, though it needs sun in order to keep its colour. In dull, shady places it turns to a pleasant light green. There are variegated types such as *L. ovalifolium* 'Argenteum' which has cream-edged leaves and *L.o.* 'Aureum', which has yellow-edged leaves. All keep their leaves throughout the winter and are invaluable in difficult situations.

Aucuba japonica is another heavy-duty plant which will bring green vitality to poor corners. It has been so abused because of its amiability that it went out of fashion, but is now coming back into favour because its handsome leaves are so useful in flower arranging. Aucubas actually prefer light shade, though the fine gold-spotted varieties need more sun than the plain green species. *Fatsia japonica* is such a handsome plant that it can be planted in a focal position in shady sheltered gardens. It has huge leathery palmate green leaves which need a protected situation in order to stay undamaged by winter gales.

Elaeagnus pungens is a quiet background plant, most useful where thick growth is required. *E.p.* 'Maculata' is more often grown for its daffodil-yellow leaves which brighten up the winter garden. However, in some situations they may be too bright, so do not plant it except as part of a planned scheme, where it will draw the eye of all beholders. *Prunus lusitanica*, the Portugal laurel, is best in large gardens where it can be grown as hedging (prune with secateurs, not shears, so as to avoid cutting the leaves in half). *Prunus laurocerasus* is the common or cherry laurel which has a cast-iron constitution. Like privet, it was used and abused in so-called 'shrubberies' in Victorian suburbia, but it and its many cultivars are both useful and beautiful whether grown for hedging, screening, background shrubs or as specimens.

Pittosporum tenuifolium is a flower-arranger's plant, with small, dainty, waved pale green leaves and black stems. It is not totally hardy. *Choisya ternata*, the Mexican orange, is a very ornamental plant with rosettes of shining leaves. This plant is so attractive that it should be used in moderation so that it can embellish an otherwise dull area of brick, stone or concrete, (or other, plainer plants). It is best in a sheltered position, and has aromatic (when squeezed) foliage. *Rhododendron ponticum* can be used as hedging and as screening or shelter,

[Text continues on p. 32

The blue-painted railings are a pleasing and unusual colour among the many greens of the surrounding foliage.

Eucalyptus, *Physocarpus opulifolius* 'Lutea' and *Prunus cerasifera* 'Pissardii' form a pleasing summer–long colour contrast in the author's small garden.

but it will grow exceedingly large exceedingly quickly; it can be moved quite easily in maturity, though not in dry weather nor in full bloom. *Viburnum tinus* (formerly *Laurustinus*) is a pleasant evergreen that will 'oblige' almost anywhere, even in dry shade, or under the drip of trees, though like most plants it will do better in more suitable conditions.

Hebes are very good in coastal gardens, disregarding strong winds that often carry sand. There are a tremendous number of varieties, many with leaves other than green (see Chapter 5). They are not hardy in cold areas, so do not get to love them too much as funerals can be frequent.

Tamarisk, *Tamarix pentandra*, is a pleasing light green colour with feathery branches that make a soft background to other more solid plants, or it can be planted to soften hard outlines, or used as a contrast plant in its own right. It likes the wind in its hair and sand between its toes but does not tolerate lime.

Lonicera nitida, the shrubby honeysuckle, is a neat-leaved shrub that can be used as hedging or as a specimen plant. The green-leaved species plant does well and uncomplainingly in shade, but the yellow-leaved variety *L.n.* 'Baggesen's Gold' needs sun in order to stay yellow; branches of it are eternally and beautifully useful in flower arrangements.

Griselinia littoralis, with its distinctive pale green leathery leaves is a plumply handsome shrub when grown inland in a sheltered place, though it may well perish in cold, wet winters. Conversely, it does well in maritime areas, though here it is often somewhat scorched or scarified by sand-bearing sea winds, and may not always look its best.

These are some of the more useful and easy shrubs to use as backgrounds, screens or 'garden-dividers' and a sharp eye when garden visiting will yield more, though it is always as well to check on the plant's preferences and hardiness.

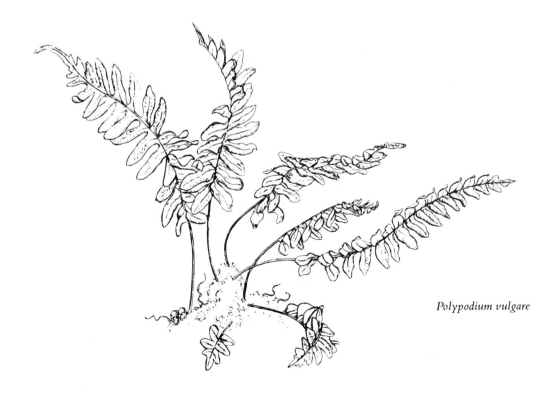

Polypodium vulgare

5

OTHER THAN GREEN

This is where the foliage garden is fun. There are so many leaves which come in colours other than green that planning and planting with them is like using a large, three-dimensional paint brush.

Yellow and gold foliage

Yellow or gold leaves brighten any garden and look spectacular when seen against a thunderous sky. But do not have too many of them where they can all be seen at once, or the garden (or this part of it) may look as though bleached. The exception to this is in a collector's garden; he may well prefer to have nothing else but tones of yellow. Fuller details of height, habit, spread and so on appear in the alphabetical list in Chapter 7.

Trees
Acer cappadocicum 'Aureum'; *Acer saccharinum* 'Lutescens'; *Gleditschia triacanthos* 'Sunburst'; *Ilex aquifolium* 'Flavescens'; *Laurus nobilis* 'Aurea'; *Robinia pseudoacacia* 'Frisia'; *Sorbus aria* 'Aurea'.

Shrubs
Berberis thunbergii 'Aurea'; *Calluna vulgaris* 'Aurea', 'Beoley Gold' and 'Gold Haze'; *Corylus avellana* 'Aurea'; *Erica carnea* 'Aurea'; *Fuchsia* 'Genii'; *Hebe ochracea*; *Ilex aquifolium flavescens*; *Ligustrum ovalifolium* 'Aureum' (golden privet); *Lonicera nitida* 'Baggesen's Gold'; *Philadelphus coronarius* 'Aureus'; *Physocarpus opulifolius* 'Luteus'; *Sambucus racemosa plumosa* 'Aurea'; *Spiraea bumalda* 'Goldflame'; *Thymus citriodorus* 'Aureus' (golden thyme); *Weigela* 'Looymansii Aurea'.

Climbers
Hedera helix 'Buttercup'; *Humulus lupulus* 'Aureus' (golden hop).

Conifers
Chamaecyparis lawsoniana 'Golden King', 'Lutea' and 'Lutea Nana'; *Chamaecyparis pisifera* 'Golden Mop' and 'Plumosa Aurea'; *Cupressus macrocarpa* 'Donard Gold'; *Juniperus* 'Pfitzerana Aurea'; *Taxus baccata* 'Dovastonii Aurea'; *Thuja occidentalis* 'Rheingold'.

Grasses, sedges and bamboos
Arundinaria viridistriata (syn. *A. auricoma*); *Carex morrowii* 'Aurea Variegata'; *Carex stricta* (Bowles' golden sedge); *Milium effusum* 'Aureum' (Bowles' golden grass).

Herbaceous plants
Filipendula ulmaria 'Aurea' (golden-leaved meadow sweet); *Hosta fortunei* 'Aurea'; *Lamium maculatum* 'Aureum'; *Lysimachia nummularia* 'Aurea' (creeping Jenny); *Melissa officinalis* 'All Gold'; *Origanum vulgare* 'Aureum' (yellow marjoram); *Saxifraga moschata* 'Cloth of Gold'; *Solidago* 'Goldenmosa'.

[Text continues on p. 37

A collection of mature hostas, as seen here gives some indication of their handsomely sculptural leaves. There are now very many kinds and colours from which to choose.

The simplicity of these grey stone steps and the wall behind is enhanced by clipped yews, the perfect harmony of ivy and conifers and the fine foliage of the tree peony.

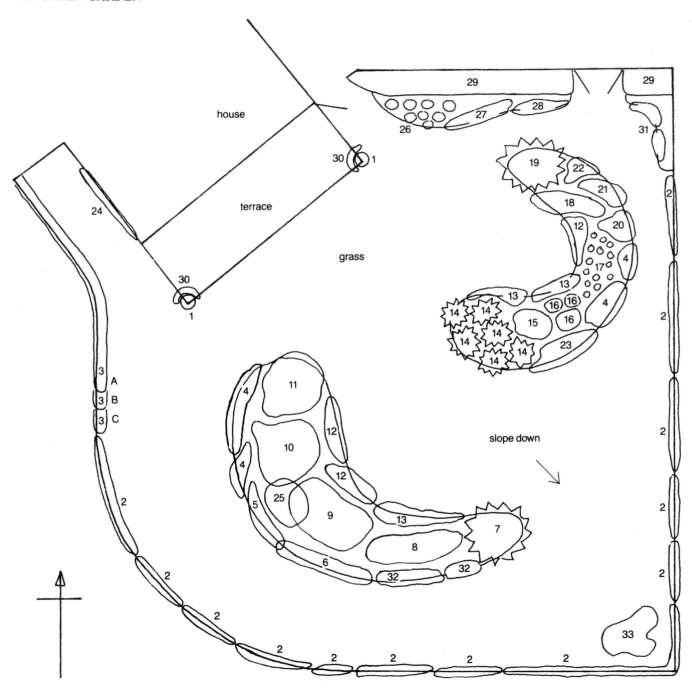

Fig. 5. The Sunny, Hot, Dry Garden

This kind of garden usually has good drainage where sun-loving plants flourish. It slopes down to a low wall, covered with a collection of variegated hederas. There is a further drop to the road.

1. Cordylines or Helichrysum petiolatum in tall urns
2. Collection of variegated Hederas
3. Taxus hedge (for privacy, stepped down at A, B, C)
4. Stachys lanata 'Silver Carpet'
5. Ajuga
6. Origanum vulgare 'Aureum'
7. Cynara scolymus
8. Amaranthus 'Joseph's Coat'
9. Weigela florida 'Foliis Purpureis'
10. Abies concolor 'Glauca compacta'
11. Rosa rubrifolia
12. Bergenia
13. Alchemilla
14. Kniphofias
15. Lonicera 'Baggesen's Gold'
16. Atriplex hortensis 'Rubra'
17. Cannas
18. Santolina
19. Trachycarpus
20. Ballota
21. Berberis thunbergii 'Atropurpurea Nana'
22. Elaeagnus 'Silver Queen'
23. Anthemis cupaniana
24. Actinidia
25. Curtonus paniculatus
26. Melianthus major
27. Cotinus coggygria
28. Artemisia ludoviciana
29. Escallonia hedge
30. Rosmarinus lavandulaceus
31. Ruta
32. Sedum spectabile
33. Natural sculpture with Hedera helix 'Sagittaefolia'

Red, crimson, purple and bronze foliage

Red, crimson, purple and the bronze tones of all these are very dramatic, therefore use them sparingly for greater impact and site them carefully for all-round interest. Small groups of toning shades are pleasing, but be moderate or the effect will be lost. Too large a grouping of this colour scheme can be sombre.

Trees

Acer palmatum 'Atropurpureum' and 'Dissectum Variegatum'; *Fagus sylvatica* 'Purpurea' or 'Riversii'; *Malus* × 'Profusion' and Malus × 'Purpurea'; *Pittosporum tenuifolium* 'Purpureum'; *Prunus cerasifera* 'Pissardii' and 'Nigra'; *Quercus robur* 'Atropurpurea'.

Shrubs

Acer palmatum 'Dissectum Atropurpureum'; *Berberis thunbergii* 'Atropurpurea' and 'Atropurpurea Nana'; *Corylus maxima* 'Purpurea'; *Cotinus coggygria* 'Royal Purple'; *Fuchsia magellanica* 'Versicolor'; *Phormium tenax* 'Purpureum'; *Photinia fraseri* 'Red Robin'; *Pieris* 'Forest Flame'; *Salvia* 'Purpurescens'; *Sambucus nigra* 'Purpurea'; *Weigela florida* 'Foliis Purpurea'.

Climbers

Vitis vinifera 'Purpurea'.

Annuals and perennials

Antirrhinums such as *A.* 'Black Prince; *Astilbe* 'Irrlicht', and 'Red Light', *A. crispa* 'Perkeo' and *A. simplicifolia* 'Sprite'; *Atriplex hortensis* 'Purpurea'; *Begonia semperflorens* – bronze-leaved varieties; *Dahlia* 'Bishop of Llandaff'; *Dianthus barbatus* (sweet William) – crimson-flowered varieties; *Erica carnea* (syn. *E. herbacea*) 'Ruby Glow' and 'Vivellii'; *Erica cinerea* 'Atrosanguinea'; *Erica mediterranea* 'Rubra'; *Rheum palmatum* 'Rubra'; *Ricinus communis* 'Gibsonii' and 'Impala'; *Sedum maximum* 'Atropurpureum'; *Sempervivum* 'Atropurpureum', 'Othello', 'Royal Ruby' and 'Rubin'; *Viola labradorica*.

Green with white or cream variegations

The sparkle of variegation is like the flicker of sunshine and shadow – it brings the garden to life. Variegated foliage, whether it be green and white or green and cream, or a mixture of both, needs to be planted in isolation or its charm is lost through like association.

Trees

Acer negundo 'Variegatum'; *Cornus controversa* 'Variegata'; *Crataegus monogyna* 'Variegata'; *Fraxinus pennsylvanica* 'Variegata'; *Ilex* – many varieties, see Chapter 7; *Quercus robur* 'Variegata'.

Shrubs

Acer palmatum 'Albomarginatum'; *Aralia elata* 'Variegata'; *Cornus alba* 'Elegantissima'; *Euonymus fortunei* 'Silver Queen'; *Griselinia littoralis* 'Variegata'; *Hebe* × *andersonii* 'Variegata'; *Pachysandra terminalis* 'Variegata'; *Philadelphus coronarius* 'Variegatus'; *Pieris japonica* 'Variegata'; *Pittosporum tenuifolium* 'Silver Queen'; *Rubus microphyllus* 'Variegatus'; *Sambucus nigra* 'Albovariegata'; *Vinca major* 'Variegata'; *Vinca minor* 'Variegata'; *Weigela florida* 'Variegata'.

Climbers

Hedera – many varieties, see Chapter 7.

Conifers

Chamaecyparis lawsoniana 'Argenteovariegata'; *Juniperus* × *media* 'Albovariegata'.

Herbaceous plants

Arum italicum 'Pictum'; *Hosta* 'Thomas Hogg'; *Hosta ventricosa* 'Variegata'; *Iris pallida* 'Variegata'; *Lamium* 'Beacon Silver'; *Lamium galeobdolon* (now *Lamiastrum galeobdolon*); *Lunaria annua* 'Variegata'; *Pulmonaria saccharata* and its variety 'Argentea'.

Green with yellow or gold variegations

The variegated plants in sunny gold or yellow are just that – they bring permanent sunshine to the garden even on dull, wet days. But be sparing with them, as too many, too close together will make that part of the garden look as if diseased.

Trees

Acer pseudoplatanns 'Leopoldii'; *Fagus sylvatica* 'Luteovariegata'; *Ilex* – many varieties, see Chapter 7; *Liriodendron tulipifera* 'Aureomarginatum';*Buxus sempervirens* 'Aurea Pendula'.

Shrubs

Aucuba japonica 'Gold Dust', *Daphne odora* 'Aureomarginata'; *Elaeagnus pungens* 'Maculata'; *Euonymus* 'Emerald 'n' Gold'; *Ilex* – many varieties; *Osmanthus* 'Aureomarginatus'; *Salvia* 'Icterina'; *Syringa emodi* 'Aureovariegata'.

Climbers

Hedera colchica 'Paddy's Pride'; *Hedera helix* 'Goldheart'; *Jasminum officinale* 'Aureovariegatum'; *Lonicera japonica* 'Aureoreticulata'.

Conifers

Chamaecyparis lawsoniana 'Aureovariegata'; *Juniperus* × *media* 'Aureovariegata'.

Bamboos

Arundinaria viridistriata; *Sasa veitchii*.

Herbaceous plants

Hosta fortunei 'Aurea Marginata'; *Saxifraga umbrosa* 'Variegata'; *Tolmiea menziesii* 'Maculata'.

Grey, white and silver foliage

There are many tones of grey, white or silver-foliaged plants; all need sunny sites to thrive. As with the other 'contrast' colours, use them sparingly and not all together, unless a silver and white garden is planned.

Trees

Eucalyptus spp.; *Populus alba canescens*; *Pyrus salicifolia* 'Pendula'; *Pyrus* × *canescens*; *Salix alba* 'Sericea'; *Salix exigua*.

Shrubs

Artemisia abrotanum; *Artemisia absinthium* and its variety 'Lambrook Silver'; *Artemisia arborescens*; *Artemisia ludoviciana*; *Artemisia schmidtiana* 'Nana'; *Ballota pseudodictamnus*; *Buddleia alternifolia* 'Argentea'; *Calluna vulgaris* 'Silver Queen'; *Caryopteris* × *clandonensis incana*; *Cistus* × *canescens*; *Cistus* × *glaucus*; *Convolvulus cneorum*; *Cytisus battandieri*; *Dorycnium hirsutum*; *Elaeagnus commutata*; *Euryops acraeus*; *Hebe pinguifolia* 'Pagei'; *Helianthemum nummularium* 'The Bride'; *Helichrysum* (many); *Hippophae rhamnoides*; *Lavandula spica* 'Hidcote' and others; *Lavandula stoechas*; *Leptospermum cunninghamii*; *Olearia* × *scilloniensis*; *Perovskia atriplicifolia*; *Romneya* (all); *Salix lanata*; *Santolina chamaecyparissus*; *Senecio greyi*.

Conifers

Abies 'Glauca Compacta'; *Cedrus atlantica glauca*; *Chamaecyparis lawsoniana* 'Pembury Blue'; *Chamaecyparis pisifera* 'Boulevard' and 'Squarrosa'; *Juniperus chinensis* 'Grey Owl'; *Juniperus* × *media* 'Pfitzerana Glauca'.

Herbaceous and other plants

Acaena adscendens, *Acaena* 'Blue Haze'; *Achillea argentea*; *Alyssum saxatile*; *Anaphalis triplinervis*; *Anthemis cupaniana*; *Artemisia glacialis*; *Cerastium tomentosum* and 'Columnae'; *Cynara scolymus*; *Dianthus* (almost all); *Dicentra* 'Langtrees'; *Eryngium* (many); *Festuca amethystina* (glauca); *Lychnis coronaria* (rose campion); *Onopordon acanthium*; *Potentilla anserina*; *Saxifraga* (many); *Sedum* (many); *Sempervivum* (many); *Senecio leucostachys*; *Senecio* 'White Diamond'; *Stachys lanata* 'Silver Carpet'; *Tanacetum densum amani* (syn. *Chrysanthemum haradjanii*).

Blue foliage

There are several conifers which have a distinct blue tinge to their needles, as well as the following shrubs and perennials: *Cheiranthus* 'Bowles Mauve'; *Echinops ritro* (globe thistle); *Eryngium* (many); *Hosta sieboldiana elegans*; *Kniphofia caulescens*; *Rosa rubrifolia*; *Ruta* 'Jackman's Blue'; *Sedum* (many).

Black foliage

The only plant which can truly be described as almost black is *Ophiopogon planiscapus nigrescens*.

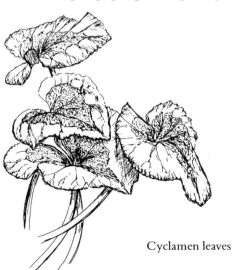

Cyclamen leaves

6

THE LAZY, BUSY OR ABSENTEE GARDENER

The pressures of modern living mean that precious time, better spent, is used up in travelling to work and travelling home again, after which the gardener is too tired to do anything much that entails effort, though he – or she – needs a neat, smart garden to show off when friends come to call. There are two hurdles to face in this situation: one is that, initially, some holiday time *must* be spent purchasing and planting things (ask a garden-clever friend to come with you and take most but not all of their advice). After this the garden will *almost* look after itself but not quite – it must, occasionally, be watered in dry spells, though you may be able to come to some arrangement with a neighbour about this. I have a builder friend with a very neat and attractive garden. He hates gardening and does absolutely no gardening at all, his neighbours taking in turns to see to his plants, do his watering and autumn clearing, while he happily fixes their taps, mends their gutters, replaces doors, windows, chimneys, roof-tiles and re-cements their paths and steps. It is a very excellent and harmonious arrangement which came about because his neighbours couldn't tolerate the untidiness of his garden between their manicured patches. Failing this state of perfect job-sharing, one must do it oneself, and the secret is to choose strong, sturdy plants that are not too invasive. The idea is to look neat and tidy for very long periods, so set the plants out (in damp weather), water them in and feed them as you do so and the garden will then be a credit to you (and to me). Thereafter, use an appropriate weedkiller occasionally, reading the instructions at least twice. It will take less than an hour to find the tin or bottle, read the instructions, mix up

the nostrum, water it on and wash out the can or other vessel. This takes a great deal less time than the kind of weeding that other, more dedicated gardeners actually enjoy. The selection of well-behaved plants is, necessarily, more limited, but what would you? You cannot have it both ways. Settle for these and prepare to receive the odd compliment from your startled friends who know that you dislike or are too 'busy' to see to the garden.

The same circumstances apply to the absentee gardener, who may have a weekend cottage or ground-floor flat that does not get weekended in as often as planned. This is a slightly different set of circumstances – this gardener may really *like* plants and gardens but may be prevented from playing at mud pies because of absence. Watering in dry spells is also a problem here, but it may be possible to make an arrangement with a neighbour or local friend which, in any case, is a very good thing to do as it kills two birds with one watering can – this invaluable person can keep a closer eye on your property and at the same time scarecrow away the burglars.

In either case, keep the plan and the planting simple and unfussed. Have paving instead of grass, but not gravel, unless you are prepared to dose it with weed-killer. Gravel is a perfect cultural area for seedlings of all kinds, moss will form in it and dead leaves will fall on it in autumn, so it, too, needs attention which it might not receive. Paving is a once-only cost, expensive at the time but long-lasting and beautiful for ever.

If the garden is sunny, choose real sun-lovers. If shaded and/or damp, select plants that like these condi-

[Text continues on p. 44

Fig. 6.   The Lazy, Busy or Absentee Gardener

This garden does not quite look after itself, but it is high in low maintenance. It will repay irregular and spasmodic care by looking permanently neat.

1. Weigela florida 'Foliis Purpureis'
2. Cornus alba 'Elegantissima'
3. Thuja 'Rheingold'
4. Berberis thunbergii 'Atropurpurea'
5. Montbretia
6. Bergenia
7. Yuccas
8. Origanum vulgare 'Aureum'
9. Alchemilla
10. Griselinia
11. Rhus typhina
12. Myrrhis odorata
13. Galium odoratum
14. Tamarix
15. Euonymus 'Emerald 'n Gold'
16. Hedera
17. Genista aetnensis
18. Pittosporum tenuifolium
19. Artemisia ludoviciana
20. Geranium endressii or G. macrorrhizum
21. Cotinus coggygria
22. Ligustrum – variegated or gold
23. Ajuga
24. Aucubas
25. Chamaecyparis pisifera 'Boulevard'
26. Dianthus or Cerastium or Nepeta
27. Hydrangea petiolaris or Akebia quinata

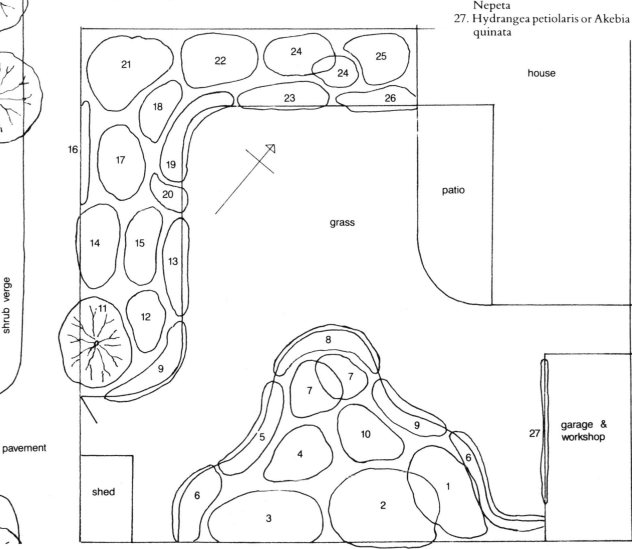

41

Light coloured grassy foliage illuminates a darker corner and makes a satisfying contrast in colour and texture between the tree trunk and the paved path.

A silver-leaved perennial is used in this hot corner to contrast with the phormium which is equally at home.

tions. Have evergreens (or evergreys) as their leaves (mostly) stay put in a neat and tidy fashion. Leave sufficient growing space between the plants so that you will seldom have to face the task of removing a too-exuberant shrub. Choose easy ground-cover plants that will spread quietly, though there will be a bramble seedling or two to eradicate from time to time. Birds will be birds. The garden plan may be of help.

Bamboo

7

THE FOLIAGE PLANTS, AN A–Z

It is not possible in a book of this size to include all the plants that I would like to see in this section, but there is a fair representation here.

Each plant is given a **descriptive code**: A = annual; Bam = bamboo; Bi = biennial; Cl = climber; Cor = corm; D = deciduous; E = evergreen; F = fern; Gr = grass; HHA = half hardy annual; HHB = half hardy biennial; HHP = half hardy perennial; HP = hardy perennial; LC = low growing carpeter; P = perennial; Rh = rhizome; Sh = shrub; Suc = succulent, T = tree; THP = tender houseplant; Tu = tuber.

Propagation methods are also coded, as follows: C = cuttings; Div = division; G = graft; L = Layers; Off = offsets; R = runners; S = seed.

Where plants, usually shrubs, are described as dioecious, the male and female flowers are produced on different plants, so both sexes will have to be grown in order for berries to form.

ABIES
A. concolor 'Glauca compacta' grows very slowly to 90 cm (3 ft) with grey-blue needle foliage. Sh/E   S or C

ACAENA
A. adscendens grows to 13 cm (5 in) with filigree blue-grey leaves. All are good for carpeting or edging; some are more invasive than others. LC/D   L

A. 'Blue Haze' 8 cm (3 in) is even more delicate, with pewter grey to mauve foliage. LC/D   L

A. microphylla 5 cm (2 in) has tiny beautiful bronze-green leaves, red burrs in summer. LC/E   Div

ACANTHUS
A. mollis grows to 1.2 m (4 ft) with purple, white and green flower stems to 1.8 m (6 ft) or more. Handsomely huge bright green, glossy, deeply cut leaves. Prefers rich soil and sun, flowers less or not at all in shade. Vanishes temporarily in hard winters. HP   Div

ACER
A. cappadocicum 'Aureum' grows to 9 m (30 ft) and spreads to 4.5 m (15 ft). The beautiful juvenile 'marbled' foliage is yellow, later turning green and then yellow again in autumn. T/D   S

A. palmatum 'Albomarginatum' grows to 4.5 m (15 ft), spreads to 2.5 m (8 ft) with smaller green, white-edged leaves. Prune all reversions. Sh/D   G

A.p. 'Atropurpureum' grows to 4.5 m (15 ft), spreads to 2.5 m (8 ft). Bronze-crimson 'maple' leaves, can be badly burnt by late frosts: plant in sheltered position. Sh/D   G

A.p. 'Dissectum Atropurpureum' deeply divided purple leaves. Frost tender. Sh/D   G

A. pseudoplatanus 'Leopoldii' grows to 9 m (30 ft), spreads to 4.5 m (15 ft). Juvenile foliage yellow-pink, later green with yellow and pink speckles and splashes. T/D   G

A. saccharinum 'Lutescens' grows to over 9 m (30 ft), spreads to 4.5 m (15 ft) or more. Foliage yellow-green. Sh/D   G

ACTINIDIA
A. kolomikta grows to 6 m (20 ft). Tricoloured, heart-shaped foliage of cream, green and pink. Best in warm, sheltered position. Flowers white. Needs good, well-drained soil, not chalky. Cl/D   C and S

AEGOPODIUM
A. podagraria 'Variegatum' (variegated ground elder)

grows to 23 cm (9 in) with handsome green and white leaves. Well-behaved and good-looking cousin to the dreadful weed. White flowers. HP   Div

AILANTHUS

A. altissima (tree of heaven). Fast-growing to 30 m (100 ft), with dissected leaves 1 m (3 ft) long. Dioecious. Female trees produce large clusters of reddish pods. T/D   S

AJUGA

A. reptans 'Atropurpurea' (or 'Purpurea') grows to 10 cm (4 in) with shining purple rosetted foliage. Spreads quickly by means of runners. Evergreen in mild areas, needs sun. Blue flowers in spring. LC/E   Div

A. reptans 'Burgundy Glow' grows to 10 cm (4 in) with rose to crimson-magenta cream-edged leaves. Sun and good drainage. Blue flowers in spring. LC/E   Div

AKEBIA

A. quinata grows to 12 m (40 ft) with beautiful foliage composed of five rounded leaflets, bronzed juvenile growth. Scented crimson flowers in spring. Cl/semiE   L

ALCHEMILLA

A. alpina grows to 13 cm (5 in) with palmate green leaves, edged and backed with silver. HP   Div

A. mollis grows to 45 cm (18 in), with very beautiful semi-circular pleated leaves and sprays of tiny lime yellow flowers in summer. HP   Div or S

AMARANTHUS

A. tricolor 'Joseph's Coat' grows to 90 cm (3 ft) with astonishing foliage in shades of scarlet, crimson, yellow, bronze and green. Red 'brushy' flowers in late summer. HHA   S

ANGELICA

A. archangelica (the angelica of cookery) grows to 1.8 m (6 ft) with yellow-green leaves and large spherical umbels of green flowers. Plant in small groups. Bi   S

ANTHEMIS

A. cupaniana grows to 30 cm (12 in), spreads to 1 m (3 ft) with foaming billows of grey-green, finely dissected foliage and white daisy flowers. HP   C/Div

ANTIRRHINUM

A. majus vars. (snapdragon). Can be chosen in various heights from pygmy size to 1.2 m (4 ft). 'Black Prince' has dark crimson leaves, as does 'Black Knight'. HHB   S

ARALIA

A. elata 'Variegata' (Japanese angelica tree). A large suckering shrub grows to 4.5 m (15 ft) or more with cream-edged green leaves and puffs of creamy flowers in autumn. Sh/D   G

ARAUCARIA

A. araucana (monkey puzzle) grows to over 24 m (80 ft) with instantly recognizable branches consisting of overlapping scales. Planted as an ornamental in Victorian times, several avenues of these interesting trees still exist in parts of the British Isles. Plant as an isolated specimen or in a small, well-separated group. T/E   S

ARTEMISIA

A. abrotanum (southernwood, lad's love) grows to 1.2 m (4 ft) with soft, aromatic, dissected grey-green foliage. Reduce stems in spring when new growth starts. Needs sun. Sh/D   C

A. absinthium (wormwood) grows to 90 cm (3 ft), spreads to 90 cm (3 ft) with dissected grey foliage. 'Lambrook Silver' is even more silvery. Sh/D   C

A. ludoviciana (white sage) grows to 1.2 m (4 ft), spread is infinite. Lovely silver-white willow-like leaves, dreadful brownish flowers. Forgivably invasive. HP   Div

A. schmidtiana 'Nana' grows to a 15 cm (6 in) mound with soft silver, finely dissected foliage. Tender. Leave stems on in winter and protect in cold areas. Sh/D   C

ARUM

A. italicum 'Pictum' grows to 45 cm (18 in) with very handsome green and ivory leaves in winter. These disappear in late summer. Berries on red stems in autumn. Tu   Div

ARUNCUS

A. sylvester (syn. *auricoma*) grows to 1.8 m (6 ft) with bronze juvenile foliage, very like that of an astilbe. Best in damp soil but will grow in border conditions. Creamy, fluffy plumes in summer. HP   Div

ARUNDINARIA

A. nitida (bamboo) grows to 3 m (10 ft) with purplish stems of bright green leaves. Invasive, and needs its space. Bam/E   Div

A. viridistriata grows to 1.2 m (4 ft) with yellow and green leaves. Cut down in spring for bright new growth. Bam/E   Div

ASPARAGUS
A. sprengeri grows to 30 cm (12 in), spreads to 1.2 m (4 ft). A tender houseplant, with sheaves of thorny, light green foliage or phylloclades. Set out in shady situations in summer, water and feed well. THP   Div or S

ASPERULA
A. odorata (sweet woodruff) grows to 10 cm (4 in) and spreads widely. Neat whorls of green leaves throughout the summer. White flowers in late spring. Good in semi-shade as edging or as ground-cover. Dried leaves smell deliciously of hay. HP   Div

ASTILBE
Many species and varieties. Juvenile foliage usually bronze, some varieties retain this colour, notably *A.* 'Irrlicht', white flowers, 50 cm (20 in); *A.* 'Red Light', red flowers, 25 cm (10 in); *A.* × *crispa* 'Perkeo', pink flowers, 25 cm (10 in); *A. simplicifolia* 'Sprite', shell pink flowers, 25 cm (10 in) and *A. simplicifolia* 'Bronze Elegance', pale salmon flowers, 30 cm (12 in). All have beautiful fern-like foliage and associate well with hostas, rodgersias, irises and other moisture-loving plants. Best in partial shade and rich damp soil. HP   Div

ATRIPLEX
A. hortensis 'Rubra' grows to 1.2 m (4 ft) with crimson-purple foliage. A   S

AUCUBA
A. japonica grows to 3.6 m (12 ft), spreads to 2.1 m (7 ft) or more. A very useful shrub for shaded places. Male and female plants needed for red winter berries. The variety 'Gold Dust' (female) is particularly good, with leaves splashed and speckled with yellow. *A. j.* 'Variegata' or 'Maculata' can look similar. Sh/E   C or S

BALLOTA
B. pseudodictamnus grows to 60 cm (2 ft), spread similar. Grey-white felted leaves. Tiny greenish white artificial-looking flowers in summer. Tender, needs sun and a sheltered site. Protect in winter. Sh/E   C

BERBERIS
B. darwinii grows to 3 m (10 ft) with a similar spread. Small, glossy, prickly leaves. Masses of golden yellow flowers in spring, followed by blue fruits. Sh/E   C

B. × *ottawensis* 'Purpurea' grows to 2.5 m (8 ft) with rich wine-purple foliage. Yellow flowers. Sh/D   C

B. thunbergii 'Atropurpurea' grows to over 1.8 m (6 ft) with a similar spread. Purple-red foliage. Sh/D   C

B. t. 'Nana' grows only to 45 cm (18 in) and is better for small gardens. Sh/D   C

B. t. 'Aurea Nana' grows to 60 cm (2 ft) with a similar spread. Yellow-green foliage, turning to pale green in late summer. Sh/D   C

B. t. 'Red Chief' has upright branches clothed with wine-red foliage. Sh/D   C

BERGENIA
B. cordifolia grows to 30 cm (12 in) with handsome deep green leathery leaves. Will grow almost anywhere except in a bog. Pink flowers in spring. HP/E   Div

BRASSICA
Ornamental cabbage and kale can be a most unexpected, unusual and striking addition to a foliage garden. The plants come in shades of pink, carmine and cream. A   S

BUDDLEIA
B. alternifolia grows to 6 m (20 ft) with a similar spread. Can be grown as a bush or as a standard tree. Silvery, hairy leaves and pendulous branches. Lavender flowers in summer. Sh/D   C

BUXUS
B. sempervirens grows to 3 m (10 ft) with small neat green leaves. Eternal and good-natured. Sh/E   C

B.s. 'Suffruticosa' is dwarf – 30 cm (1 ft) if kept trimmed – and much used for low hedging. Sh/E   C

CALLUNA
All heathers are best in genuinely acid, moisture-retentive, humus-rich soil and full sun. Sh/E   C

C. vulgaris 'Aurea' grows to 30 cm (1 ft) with golden foliage turning to red in winter. Purple flowers.

C.v. 'Beoley Gold' grows to 45 cm (18 in) with golden yellow foliage and white flowers.

C.v. 'Gold Haze' grows to 60 cm (2 ft) with yellow foliage and white flowers.

C.v. 'Orange Queen' grows to 60 cm (2 ft) with gold foliage changing to deep orange. Pink flowers.

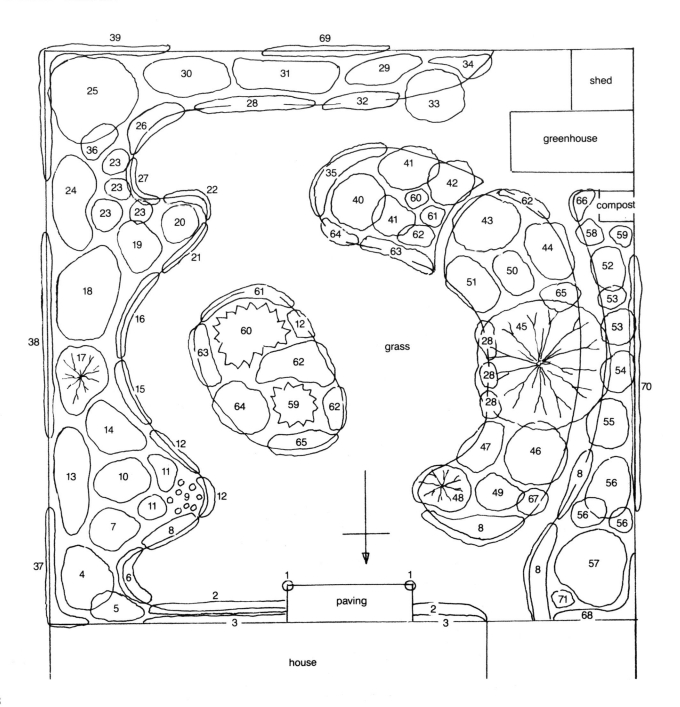

house

Fig. 7. The Suburban Garden

The shape may be dictated by the area but the garden need not be. This plan shows a garden with secrets. The island bed could be a pond with appropriate bog and water-plants, or it may be dedicated to heathers if the soil is acid. (See also p. 17.)

1. Pelargoniums
2. Nepeta
3. Iris
4. Choisya
5. Fuchsia magellanica 'Versicolor'
6. Sedum
7. Lavandula
8. Bergenia
9. Cannas
10. Macleaya
11. Lonicera 'Baggesen's Gold'
12. Ajuga
13. Tamarix
14. Olearia macrodonta
15. Dianthus
16. Lysimachia nummularia 'Aurea'
17. Paulownia
18. Cornus alba 'Elegantissima'
19. Berberis thunbergii 'Atropurpurea'
20. Conifer, Taxus or Pinus mugo
21. Heuchera
22. Cerastium
23. Verbascums
24. Weigela florida 'Foliis Purpureis'
25. Bamboo
26. Alchemilla
27. Anthemis cupaniana
28. Hostas
29. Pittosporum tenuifolium
30. Amaranthus 'Joseph's Coat'
31. Spiraea × bumalda 'Goldflame'
32. Elaeagnus 'Silver Queen'
33. Taxus 'Dovastonii Aurea'
34. Lunaria
35. Artemisia ludoviciana
36. Foeniculum
37. Hedera
38. Clematis armandii
39. Humulus lupulus 'Aureus'
40. Pyrus salicifolius 'Pendula'
41. Ricinus communis
42. Genista aetnensis
43. Rhus typhina
44. Griselinia
45. Ailanthus altissima or Populus alba canescens
46. Mahonias
47. Hostas
48. Robinia pseudoacacia 'Frisia'
49. Cercidiphyllum
50. Elaeagnus pungens 'Maculata'
51. Myrrhis odorata
52. Sambucus
53. Viburnums
54. Bamboo
55. Ilex
56. Aucuba
57. Fatsia japonica
58. Artemisia absinthium
59. Yuccas
60. Juniperus × media 'Pfitzerana Glauca'
61. Origanum vulgare 'Aureum'
62. Dianthus
63. Ruta
64. Alchemilla
65. Bergenia
66. Montbretia
67. Pulmonaria
68. Garrya elliptica
69. Parthenocissus henryana
70. Akebia quinata
71. Fuchsia magellanica

C.v. 'Silver Queen' grows to 60 cm (2 ft) with silvery grey foliage and pale mauve flowers.
CANNA
C. hybrida grows to 1.2 m with green, bronze and brown, purple or crimson-toned foliage. TRh   Div
CAREX
C. morrowii 'Aurea Variegata' grows to 45 cm (18 in) with green-edged, bright gold leaves. Prefers dampish soil. Gr   Div
C. pendula (pendulous sedge) grows to 90 cm (3 ft) with arching wands of green tassels. Gr/E   Div or S
C. stricta (Bowles' golden sedge) grows to 60 cm (2 ft) with striped gold and green leaves. GR   Div
CEDRUS
C. atlantica 'Glauca' (blue Atlas cedar) grows to 15 m

(50 ft) with a spread of 6 m (20 ft). Glaucous blue-green foliage. T/E   S
CERASTIUM
C. tomentosum (snow-in-summer) grows to 15 cm (6 in), spreads quickly and infinitely. Silver white leaves and white flowers. LC/E   Div
C.t. 'Columnae' grows to 10 cm (4 in) with quieter behaviour. Both are slightly tender. LC/E   Div
CERCIDIPHYLLUM
C. japonicum grows to 7.5 m (25 ft) with graceful branches of heart-shaped, almost spherical leaves. Small and inconspicuous flowers. Good autumn colour. A very lovely small tree, sometimes tender. T/D   S
CHAMAECYPARIS
C.l. 'Ellwood's Gold' (columnar) grows to 1.8 m (6 ft)

[Text continues on p. 52

49

A green garden on a large scale – beautiful contrasts in shape, colour, texture and height for year-round interest.

The pieris (*lower right*) will colour to flame-red in spring against a background of glossy green. The cotoneaster on the wall will repeat the performance in autumn.

with yellow-tipped green foliage. Sh/E   C

C.l. 'Lutea' grows to 9 m (30 ft), spreads to 1.8 m (6 ft) with pendulous golden yellow foliage sprays. T/E   C

C.l. 'Pembury Blue' grows to 6 m (20 ft) with silvery blue foliage, later turning green. T/E   C

C. pisifera 'Boulevard' grows to 4.5 m (15 ft) or more, with a spread of 3 m (10 ft). Feathery, tufty blue-silver foliage. Sh/E   C

C.p. 'Plumosa Aurea Nana' grows to only 90 cm (3 ft), spreads to 60 cm (2 ft) with bright gold fluffy foliage. This should remain throughout the year. Sh/E   C

CHAMAEPERICLYMENUM
C. canadense grows to 25 cm (10 in) with mid-green leaf rosettes, white 'flowers' and later, red berries. Best in acid soil. Slightly tender. P   Div

CHEIRANTHUS
C. 'Bowles's Mauve' grows to 75 cm (2½ ft) with grey-mauve foliage; matching flowers. Tender. HHP   C

CHOISYA
C. ternata (Mexican orange) grows to 1.8 m (6 ft) with a similar or greater spread. Good-looking, with glossy trifoliate leaves. Scented white flowers. Sh/E   C

C. t. 'Sundance' grows to 90 cm (3 ft) and is a new variety with golden leaves. Scented white flowers. (It is protected by UK Plant Breeders Rights no. 3106.) Slightly tender. Sh/E

CLEMATIS
C. armandii grows to a vigorous 9 m (30 ft) with deeply veined, glossy, trifoliate, dark green leaves; bronze new growth. White flowers in spring. Cl/E   C or S

COLEUS
C. blumei (its common name is flame nettle) Many varieties with astonishing foliage colours, including all shades of red, orange and gold as well as greens, white, pinks, even midnight blue and chocolate brown. Heights from 13 cm (5 in) to 45 cm (18 in). Greenhouse plants that can be placed out of doors in summer. Feed well and pinch out all flowers. A   C or S

CONVOLVULUS
C. cneorum grows to 90 cm (3 ft) in warm areas. Metallic silver leaves, white flowers in summer. Tender. Sh/E   C

CORDYLINE
C. indivisa grows to 6 m (20 ft) or to 1.8 m (6 ft) in a tub.

Long, narrow leaves form a spiky 'mop'. Tender. Sh/E   S, stem-sections or from suckers

CORNUS
C. alba 'Elegantissima' grows to 3m (10 ft) with cream-margined green leaves. Turns to salmon pink in autumn. Sh/D   C

C. canadensis (see *Chamaepericlymenum canadense*)

C. controversa grows to 6 m (20 ft), with cake-stand tiers of green and white foliage. Site against a darker background for best effect. Sh/D   C

COROKIA
C. cotoneaster (wire-netting bush) grows to 2.5 m (8 ft) with small, neat, polished leaves and a twiggy tangle of silver-grey branches. Not for cold areas. Minute yellow flowers. Sh/E   C

CORYLUS
C. maxima 'Purpurea' grows to 3 m (10 ft), with purple leaves. Sh/D   C

COTINUS
C. coggygria 'Atropurpureis' (smoke tree) grows to 2.4 m (8 ft) or more, with round to oval purple leaves. *C.c.* 'Foliis Purpureis' and *C.c.* 'Royal Purple' have even darker and more beautiful foliage. Puffs of smoke-like flowers in summer. Sh/D   C

COTONEASTER
Many species and varieties usually grown for their bright fruits in autumn, but most also have pleasing and distinctive foliage.

C. horizontalis (herringbone plant) grows to 60 cm (2 ft) and spreads to 2.1 m (7 ft). Characteristic fish-skeleton branch formation closely covered with glossy green leaves. White flowers in summer followed by red berries and red foliage in late autumn. Sh/D   S or C

C. microphyllus grows only to 15 cm (6 in) but spreads to 2.4 m (8 ft). Glossy dark green leaves are grey beneath. Good for ground cover. White flowers and red berries. Sh/E   C

COTULA
C. squalida grows to just 4 cm (1½ in) but spreads into space available. Tiny fern-like bronze-green leaves. LC/D   Div

CUPRESSOCYPARIS
× *C. leylandii* grows exceedingly quickly to 15 m (50 ft)

with a spread of 6 m (20 ft). Specimen trees are beautiful, unmanaged hedges are not · do not plant unless you can cope with this conifer. T/E   C

CUPRESSUS
C. macrocarpa (Monterey cypress) grows to 15 m (50 ft) and spreads to 4.5 m (15 ft). Dark green foliage. *C.m.* 'Donard Gold' has golden foliage. T/E   C

CURTONUS
C. paniculata (syn. *Antholyza paniculata*) 'Aunt Eliza' grows to 1.2 m (4 ft) with handsome, stiff, lance-shaped 'pleated' leaves. Orange montbretia-like flowers in late summer. Tender. Cor   Div

CYCLAMEN
Many species and varieties can be planted so that there are beautiful leaves for most of the year. Cor   S
C. cilicicum has rounded silver-zoned green leaves from winter onwards; pink flowers. Tender.
C. coum has mid-green leaves marked with silver from spring onwards. Pink flowers.
C. neapolitanum has very variable leaves from autumn until spring; mauve, white or pale pink flowers.

CYNARA
C. scolymus (globe artichoke) grows to 1.8 m (6 ft), with huge curving saw-toothed (but soft) silver-grey leaves. A sculptural plant. Purple flowers, beloved by bees. HP   Div or S

CYTISUS
C. battandieri grows to 3 m (10 ft) with silvery trifoliate leaves. Yellow fruit-salad-scented flowers in summer. Tender. Sh/E   C

DAHLIA (peony-flowered)
D. 'Bishop of Llandaff' grows to 90 cm (3 ft) with purple, dissected foliage. Red flowers. Rh   Div
D. 'Redskin' has maroon-bronze-green foliage and mixed flower colours. Tender. Rh   Div

DIANTHUS
D. barbatus (sweet William) grows to 20 or 60 cm (8 in to 2 ft). Crimson-flowered varieties generally have dark leaves. All have delicious scent. Bi   S
Old fashioned pinks form mats of glaucous grey-green foliage. Mixed colours. HP/E   Div or S

DICENTRA
D. eximia grows to 45 cm (18 in) with grey-green dissected foliage. Pink or white flowers. *D.* 'Langtrecs' has grey-blue foliage. HP   Div or S

DORYCNIUM
D. hirsutum grows to 60 cm, forming a mound of softly hairy, grey-green foliage. Needs sun. Sh/D   C or S

DRYOPTERIS
D. dilatata (broad buckler fern) grows to 1.2 m (4 ft). Deep green fronds. Best in moist, humus-rich soil in semi-shade. F/D   Div or spores.

ECHEVERIA
E. derenbergii grows to 4 cm (1½ in) with crown-like rosettes of bloomy, pale water-green leaves. Orange flowers. Must be cossetted in conservatory in John Innes No. 2 during winter and spring. Rescue from garden well before the frosts. Suc/E   Div

ELAEAGNUS
E. commutata (silverberry) grows to 2.5 m (8 ft) with silver leaves and berries. Beautiful. Sh/D   C
E. pungens grows to 3.6 m (12 ft) with green leaves having white undersides. *E. p.* 'Maculata' has bright gold-splashed leaves. Sh/E   C
E. p. 'Gilt Edge' has leaves margined in golden yellow and does best in full sun. Sh/E   C
E. p. 'Limelight' has leaves with a deep yellow central blotch. Sh/E   C
All elaeagnus dislike chalk.

EPIMEDIUM
All epimedium foliage is beautiful, and at its best in early summer. Remove old leaves. HP/E   Div
E. perralderianum grows to 30 cm (12 in) with bright green and bronze leaves and yellow flowers.
E. × *rubrum* has red-tinged young leaves, good autumn colour and crimson flowers.

ERICA
Ericas have many differing heights, habits and foliage colours. Sh/E   C
E. c. 'Vivellii' has bronze foliage, carmine flowers and grows to 25 cm (10 in).
E. cinerea 'Golden Drop' grows to 30 cm (12 in) with gold to copper leaves, increasing in vibrancy in winter. Sparse pink flowers.
E. tetralix 'Alba Mollis' has silver grey leaves, white flowers and grows to 30 cm (12 in).

[*Text continues on p. 56*

Astilbes, rodgersia, hostas and ferns thrive here in the dappled shade of woodland conditions.

Lysimachia nummularia 'Aurea' makes an excellent edging to this group of different hostas.

ERYNGIUM

Eryngiums have spiny bracts and a season-long metallic silver-blue sheen.

E. giganteum grows to 1.2 m (4 ft) with an overall blue, silver and ivory appearance. Bi   S

E. maritimum grows to 45 cm (18 in) with spiky silver-green leaves and green-blue flower-heads. Tender except in coastal areas. HHP   S

ESCALLONIA

Escallonias make satisfyingly dense dark hedges and backgrounds, very good in coastal areas, more tender inland. Many cultivars exist. Prune in mid or late spring if flowers are not wanted. Sh/E   C

EUCALYPTUS

There are eucalyptuses of every size for any garden. All have beautiful foliage.

E. gunnii grows to 14 m (45 ft) or more with round juvenile foliage and elongated adult leaves. Can be kept cut down as hedging, juvenile leaves will then predominate. Scented white flowers. T/E   S

EUONYMUS

E. fortunei grows to 3 m (10 ft) with glossy dark green leaves. Climbs. Sh/E   C

More often grown are *E.f.* 'Silver Queen' (60 cm (2 ft) high) with white-edged green leaves and *E.f.* 'Emerald 'n' Gold' (up to 60 cm (2 ft) high), with yellow-edged green leaves. Will climb to 1.8 m (6 ft) if a wall is handy.

EUPHORBIA

Mostly handsome, sculptural plants with (usually) green-yellow bracts.

E. cyparissias grows to 30 cm (12 in) with soft green linear foliage and lime-yellow bracts in spring. Invasive but very attractive. HP   Div

E. myrsinites grows to 15 cm (6 in) with trailing stems of pale blue-green foliage. HP   Div or S

E. wulfenii grows to 1.8 m (6 ft) with fine blue-green foliage. Needs a warm, sheltered place. HP/E   S

EURYOPS

E. acraeus can grow to 38 cm (15 in) (usually much less), with silver-grey leaves – a miniature 'palm' – and yellow flowers. Tender. Sh/E   C or S

FAGUS

Fagus sylvatica (beech) grows to 30 m (100 ft) as a tree but makes excellent hedging. *F.s.* 'Cuprea' is the copper beech. *F.s.* 'Purpurea' is the purple beech and *F.s.* 'Riversii' or 'Rivers Purple' is darker still. T or Sh/D   C

× *FATSHEDERA*

× *F. lizei* grows to 2.4 m (8 ft), spread similar. Handsome, large, leathery, glossy green palmate leaves and umbels of greenish flowers. Needs strong support. Cl/E   C

FATSIA

F. japonica grows to 4.5 m (15 ft) with huge palmate leaves and umbels of green flowers. Sh/E   C

FESTUCA

F. glauca grows to 23 cm (9 in) with glaucous blue-grey tufts of grassy foliage. Gr/E   Div

FOENICULUM

F. vulgare (fennel) grows to 2.4 m (8 ft) with hazy thread-like aromatic green foliage and yellow flowers. *F.v.* 'Purpureum' has bronze-brown foliage. HP   S

FRAXINUS

F. excelsior 'Aurea' (golden ash) grows to 18 m (60 ft) and more with golden yellow young shoots and yellow autumnal colouration. T/D   G

FUCHSIA

The variety *F.* 'Genii' has yellow foliage and red and purple flowers. Sh/D   C

F. magellanica 'Gracilis Variegata' has cream and green leaves. *F.m.* 'Versicolor' has grey, green, rose-pink, crimson and cream leaves – both have small red and purple flowers and grow to 1.2 m (4 ft). Tender. Sh/D   C

GARRYA

G. elliptica grows to 4.5 m (15 ft) with dark green leaves and grey-green catkins. Sh/E   C

GENISTA

G. aetnensis (Mt Etna broom) grows to 6 m (20 ft) with thin, airy green few-leaved branches and masses of yellow flowers. Sh/E   C

GERANIUM

G. endressii has a neat rounded mound of shining dark green leaves. Grows to 30 cm (12 in) with a diameter of 60 cm (2 ft). Pink flowers. HP   Div

G. macrorrhizum has sweet-scented, soft, pale green

leaves and pink or white flowers. Always good-looking. HP Div

G. renardii grows to 23 cm (9 in) with thick grey-green leaves and palest lilac flowers. Tender and beautiful. HHP Div

GINKGO

G. biloba grows to 9 m (30 ft) or more, with fan-shaped, pale green leaves, turning yellow in autumn. T/D S

GLEDITSCHIA

G. triacanthos 'Sunburst' (honey locust) grows to 9 m (30 ft) with sprays of yellow-green leaves, brightest in spring. T/D S

GRISELINIA

G. littoralis grows to 7.5 m (25 ft) with oval leathery, apple green leaves. G.l. 'Variegata' has green and white leaves and is tender. Sh/E C

GUNNERA

G. manicata grows to 3 m (10 ft) with spectacularly large leaves, up to 3 m (10 ft) across. Deep, moist soil essential. Not always hardy. P S

HEBE

H × andersonii 'Variegata' grows to 90 cm (3 ft) with white-edged leaves and blue flowers. Sh/E C

H. ochracea (formerly H. armstrongii) grows to 90 cm (3 ft) with 'whipcord' golden green leaves. Sh/E C

H. pagei grows to 23 cm (9 in) with glaucous grey leaves and white flowers. Sh/E C

HEDERA

H. canariensis 'Gloire de Marengo' grows to 6 m (20 ft) or more with handsome cream, grey and green leaves. Somewhat tender. Cl/E C

H. helix (common or English ivy) grows to 30 m (100 ft) with dark green leaves. Cl/E C or L

H.h. 'Buttercup' has smaller, all-yellow leaves – best in sun. Cl/E C

H.h. 'Cristata' or 'Parsley Crested' has waved and crimped edges to the light green leaves. Cl/E C

H.h. 'Glacier' has small variegated leaves in green, grey and white. Cl/E C

H.h. 'Goldheart' has green leaves with a central yellow area. Cut off all green shoots. Cl/E C

H.h. 'Sagittaefolia' has narrow, arrow-shaped green leaves. 'Variegata' has white-edged leaves. Cl/E C

H.h. 'Silver Queen' has small grey-green leaves edged with white. Cl/E C

HELICHRYSUM

H. angustifolium (curry plant) grows to 60 cm (2 ft) with pale grey leaves and yellow flowers. Can be easily pruned. Sh/E C

H. petiolatum trails to 1.2 m (4 ft) plus, with heart-shaped grey felt leaves and silver stems. Beautiful but tender. Sh/E C

HELLEBORUS

H. argutifolius (formerly H. corsicus) grows to 75 cm (2½ ft) with strong stems of pale green apparently spine-edged leaves. Green flowers. HP/E S

HELXINE

H. soleirolii (syn. Soleirolia soleirolii) (Mind your own business). Prostrate, with minute green leaves. Invasive but very useful. LC/E in mild areas Div

HIPPOPHAE

H. rhamnoides (sea buckthorn) grows to 3 m (10 ft) or more with linear silver-grey leaves and striking orange berries. Dioecious. Good in coastal areas. Sh/D S

HOSTA

There are now innumerably confusing numbers of hostas. All need humus-rich moisture-retentive soil, and most are best in partial shade. Below are just some of the old favourites. HP Div

H. albomarginata grows to 45 cm (18 in) with white-edged green leaves.

H.f. 'Aurea' has all-yellow leaves gradually turning to light green.

H.f. 'Aureomarginata' has yellow-edged green leaves. Lilac flowers.

H. sieboldiana elegans has very large blue-green leaves.

H. 'Thomas Hogg' has white-edged green leaves.

H. undulata: wavy green leaves with large areas of white.

H. ventricosa 'Variegata' has dark green leaves variegated with yellow.

Some exciting new introductions are as follows:

'Big Daddy' grows to 90 cm (3 ft) with large puckered very 'blue' leaves – full shade to partial sun.

'Blue Skies' has vivid 'blue' foliage and needs partial sun.

[Text continues on p. 60

The beauty of the grey stone walls is made even lovelier by the handsome group of conifers, with lavender in front that changes to a harmonizing grey in winter.

Luxuriant cushions of foliage grow around the base of this fountain, where delicate scallop shells catch and direct the water from an overflowing bowl above.

'Golden Medallion' (tokudama golden) grows to 50 cm (20 in) and has textured, cup-shaped golden leaves. Needs good light, even full sun.

'Golden Prayers' grows to 30 cm (12 in) and has golden leaves and mauve flowers: best in partial sun.

'Sun Power' has ruffled golden leaves. Partial sun.

'Zounds' has deeply puckered yellow leaves, good in shade, partial shade or sun.

HOUTTUYNIA

H. cordata 'Variegata' grows to 30 cm (12 in), spreads to 90 cm (3 ft) with amazing foliage of green, red and yellow. Prefers damp soil. HP   Div

HYDRANGEA

H. petiolaris grows to 18 m (60 ft) or more with light green heart-shaped leaves all turning yellow in autumn. White flowers. Cl/D   C

ILEX

I. aquifolium (holly) grows to 7.5 m (25 ft) with shining waved spiny leaves. Good as hedging, background shrubs and as specimens. Most plants are dioecious. T or Sh/E   S or C

Many varieties exist such as:

I.a. 'Flavescens', 'Clouded Gold' or 'Moonlight Holly' (female) has leaves of canary yellow, shaded with old gold. Very good in spring.

I.a. 'Golden King' (female) grows to 7.5 m (25 ft) with gold-margined leaves.

I.a. 'Silver Queen' (male) grows to 5.5 m (18 ft) and has silver-margined green leaves.

I. ferox (hedgehog holly) (male) grows slowly to 4.5 m (15 ft) and has dark green leaves with an over-abundance of pale green spines.

IRIS

Irises have excellent 'accent' foliage especially the taller 'bearded' varieties and hybrids. Rh   Div

I. pallida 'Variegata' grows to 60 cm (2 ft) with stiff, striped leaves of blue-green and white.

I. pseudacorus (yellow flag iris) has long, curving light green leaves. Generally planted in or at the edge of water but will grow in border conditions.

ITEA

I. ilicifolia grows to about 3.6 m (12 ft) with holly-like but unprickly glossy green leaves and long, scented, pale green catkins. Sh/E   C

JASMINUM

J. officinale 'Aureum' grows to 3 m (10 ft) or more with yellow-blotched green leaves. Not self-clinging. Cl/Sh/D   C

JUNIPERUS

J. communis 'Hornibrookii' (syn. 'Prostrata') grows only to 30 cm (12 in) but spreads to 1.8 m (6 ft) with grey-blue foliage. Sh/E   C

J. chinensis 'Pfitzerana' grows to 90 cm (3 ft) but spreads to 1.5 m (5 ft) with graceful drooping green branches. *J.c.* 'Pfitzerana Aurea' has gold-green foliage. Sh/E   C

J. 'Grey Owl' grows to over 4.5 m (15 ft) with soft silver-grey foliage. Sh/E   C

KNIPHOFIA

K. caulescens (red hot poker) grows to 90 cm (3 ft) with broad blue-green leaves. Late flowers of coral and yellow. Needs full sun, very well-drained soil and may require winter protection. HP/Div

KOCHIA

K. scoparia trichophylla (summer cypress) grows to 90 cm (3 ft) with vivid light green summer foliage turning brilliant red in autumn. A   S

LAMIASTRUM

L. galeobdolon 'Variegatum' (yellow archangel) grows to 60 cm (2 ft) and rampages to 6 m (20 ft) with green and black leaves splashed with silver. An excellent ground swallower for poor dry positions under trees. HP/E   R

LAMIUM

L. maculatum (dead nettle) grows to 30 cm (12 in) and spreads to 60 cm (2 ft) with mid-green leaves having a silver-white central stripe. Pink or white flowers. LC/E   Div

L.m. 'Aureum' is smaller and less robust, with yellow white-striped leaves and pink flowers.

L.m. 'Beacon Silver' has eyecatching silver leaves, but is sometimes delicate. Best in good soil and cool shade.

LAVANDULA

All the lavenders have evergreen and glaucous foliage, useful as a foil to other plants. Sh/E   C

L.spica (old English lavender) grows to 1.2 m (4 ft) with silver-grey foliage. Grey-blue flowers.

L.s. 'Hidcote' (syn. 'Nana Atropurpurea') is a more compact plant.

LIGUSTRUM
L. ovalifolium 'Argenteum' grows to 2.4 m (8 ft) green foliage edged with cream-white. Sh/E   C
L.o. 'Aureomarginatum' grows to 4.5 m (15 ft) with yellow-bordered green leaves. Sh/E   C
L. vulgare 'Aureum' has dull yellow leaves. Sh/E   C

LOBELIA
L. fulgens grows to 90 cm (3 ft) with purple-crimson foliage and scarlet flowers. *L.f.* 'Queen Victoria' is excellent. These lobelias will grow in or at the edge of water. HHP   C or Div

LONICERA
L. japonica 'Aurea reticulata' grows to 3 m (10 ft) and has oval green leaves veined with gold. Cl Sh/semi E   C
L. nitida grows to 1.8 m (6 ft) with tiny, shiny dark green leaves. Quite good in shade. 'Baggeson's Gold' has gold leaves and needs a sunny site. Sh/E   C
L. pileata has small pale green leaves and forms a pleasing mound. Will grow in tree-shade. Sh/semi E   C

LUNARIA
L. biennis (syn. *L. biennis* 'Variegata') grows to 75 cm (2½ ft) with cream-margined green leaves, best in second year. Bi   S

LYCHNIS
L. coronaria (rose campion) has silver-white furred leaves, best in the first (flowerless) year. Magenta flowers. Short lived HP   S

LYSIMACHIA
L. nummularia (creeping Jenny, moneywort) trails to 45 cm (18 in) with rounded, paired green leaves and yellow flowers, fewer in shade. Prefers damp conditions. *L.n.* 'Aurea' has yellow leaves. LC   R

MACLEAYA
M. cordata (syn. *Bocconia cordata*) (plume poppy) grows to 2.4 m (8 ft) with very beautiful jade green scalloped leaves, grey beneath, with coral-coloured veins and matching plumes of tiny flowers. This species can be confused with *M. microcarpa*. Invasive. HP   Div

MAHONIA
M. healei grows to 2.4 m (8 ft) with shiny, spiny leaflets. Sh/E   C or S

M. lomariifolia grows to 3.6 m (12 ft) with isolated stems of handsome, palm-like paired spiny leaves. Yellow flowers. Sh/E   C

MALUS
M. 'Profusion' grows to 6 m (20 ft) with bronze-green leaves and carmine flowers. T/D   G

MATTEUCCIA
M. struthiopteris (ostrich-feather fern, shuttlecock fern) grows to 1.5 m (5 ft). A beautiful fern with light green foliage, best in damp, sunny or semi-shaded situations. F   Off

MELIANTHUS
M. major grows to 1.8 m (6 ft) with very beautiful serrated grey-green leaves which smell abominable. Tender. HHP   Off

MELISSA
M.o. 'Aurea' (golden balm) has gold and green leaves. Cut back in midsummer for new growth. HP   Div

MILIUM
M. effusum 'Aureum' (Bowles' golden grass) grows to 38 cm (15 in) with pleasing yellow foliage. Best in good soil in semi-shade. Gr   Div

MISCANTHUS
M. sinensis 'Variegatus' grows to 1.8 m (6 ft) with longitudinal cream and green stripes. Gr   Div
M.s. 'Zebrinus' grows to 1.2 m (4 ft) with green leaves cross-banded in yellow. Gr   Div

MITELLA
M. breweri grows to 5 cm (2 in) with quietly spreading evergreen hummocks of crinkled dark green leaves. Always neat. Greenish flowers. HP   Div

NANDINA
N. domestica (Chinese sacred bamboo) grows to 1.8 m (6 ft) with red-toned young foliage and white flowers. Good autumn colour. Tender. Sh/D   C or S

NEPETA
N. × *faassenii* grows to a lax 45 cm (18 in), with mounds of grey-green foliage. Mauve flowers. Beautiful in quantity. Cats sometimes ravage this plant, at other times it is ignored. In my case it is the former. Tender. HP/E   Div

OLEARIA
O. macrodonta (New Zealand holly) grows to 3.6 m

[*Text continues on p. 64*

The foliage contrasts of conifer, vinca, lamiastrum and hedera will soon clothe the stonework of this rock garden.

The gentle shapes of alchemilla and geranium enhance the lichened stone steps.

(12 ft) with sage green holly-like leaves. White flowers. Sh/E   C

ONOPORDON
O. acanthium (Scotch thistle) grows to 2.5 m (8 ft), with prickly, white-silver leaves and thorny, branching stems. Purple 'thistles'. Whitest in the first year. Bi   S

OPHIOPOGON
O. planiscapus nigrescens grows to 15 cm (6 in) with striking black grass-like foliage. Pink flowers and black berries. HP   Div or S

ORIGANUM
O. vulgare 'Aureum' (golden marjoram) has sweetly aromatic golden foliage. Pink flowers. HP   Div

PACHYSANDRA
P. terminalis grows to 30 cm (12 in) and spreads to 45 cm (18 in). Rosettes of green leaves make excellent ground cover in partial shade. *P.t.* 'Variegata' has white-edged leaves and is more delicate. HP/E   Div

PARTHENOCISSUS
P. henryana (Chinese virginia creeper) grows to 9 m (30 ft) with dark green leaves having central white venation and variegation. The leaves consist of five separate leaflets. Best in semi-shade, not always hardy. Vigorous and self-clinging. Cl/D   C

P. quinquefolia (true virginia creeper) grows to 21 m (70 ft) with leaves consisting of five green leaflets that turn to brilliant shades of yellow, orange, red and crimson in autumn. Self- clinging. Cl/D   C

P. tricuspidata grows to 15 m (50 ft) with (generally) three-lobed green leaves. These turn crimson in autumn. Self-clinging. Cl/D   C

PAULOWNIA
P. tomentosa grows to 7.5 m (25 ft) with huge, soft, heart-shaped leaves. Mauve, foxglove-like flowers. Can be kept to shrub-size by pruning, which will promote larger leaves. T/D   C or S

PELTIPHYLLUM
P. peltatum grows to 1.2 m (4 ft) with huge round scalloped leaves like parasols up to 45 cm (18 in) across. Pink flowers from the bare soil in spring. Needs damp soil. Rh   Div

PERILLA
P. frutescens (syn. *nankinensis*) grows to 60 cm (2 ft) with

toothed, red-purple leaves. White flowers. *P.f.* 'Foliis Atropurpurea laciniata' is even better, with waved and more deeply cut leaves. HHA   S

PETASITES
P. japonicus 'Giganteus' (giant butter-bur) grows to 1.2 m with large round leaves appearing after green-white flowers. Needs space and damp soil. Rh   Div

PHALARIS
P. arundinacea 'Picta' (gardener's garters) grows to 60 cm (2 ft) with longitudinally striped green and white leaves (some cats like to eat these). Vigorous and spreading. Gr   Div

PHILADELPHUS
P. coronaria 'Aurea' grows to 2.7 m (9 ft) or more with bright yellow young foliage, fading to a pleasing yellow-green later on. Best in semi-shade. White flowers. Sh/D   C

PHLOMIS
P. fruticosa (Jerusalem sage) grows to 1.2 m (4 ft) with woolly grey-green leaves. Yellow flowers in whorls. Tender. Sh/E   C

PHORMIUM
P. tenax (New Zealand flax) grows to 3 m (10 ft) with fans of leathery sword-shaped leaves. Dull red flowers. Somewhat tender. There are several interesting varieties. Sh/E   Div or S

P.t. 'Purpureum' has bronze-purple foliage.

P.t. 'Variegatum' has longitudinally striped leaves in green and yellow.

Dwarf varieties, suitable for small gardens are: *P. cookianum* 'Tricolor' 1 m (3¼ ft); *P. tenax* 'Firebird', maroon leaves, edged light crimson, grows to 1 m (3¼ ft); *P.t.* 'Thumbelina' has purple-bronze leaves, and grows to only 30 cm (12 in), *P.t.* 'Yellow Wave' has golden-yellow leaves edged with green and grows to 75 cm (2½ ft). All are classified as shrubs.

PHYLLITIS
P. scolopendrium (hart's tongue fern) has light green satin ribbon-like leaves. Best in moist positions, where it grows to 60 cm (2 ft). 'Crispum' has crisply waved edges to the leaves. F/E   Div

PHYSOCARPUS
P. opulifolius 'Luteus' grows to 2.4 m (8 ft) or more with

eye-catching yellow foliage, best in early season. White flowers. Sh/D C

PICEA

P. abies 'Pumila' grows only to 60 cm (2 ft) with layered green branches. *P. abies* has several dwarf-growing varieties such as *P.a.* 'Pygmaea' which may take thirty years to reach 45 cm (18 in). Sh/E C

PIERIS

P. formosa 'Forrestii' grows to 3.6 m (12 ft) with masses of white flowers. Young growth is shining scarlet. Sh/E Div

P.f. 'Forest Flame' has brilliant red young growth, afterwards changing through pink and cream-white to green. White flowers in dangling clusters. Sh/E C

P.f. forrestii 'Wakehurst' has vivid red young foliage.

P. japonica 'Variegata' has leaves variegated first in pink which later fades to cream. Sh/E C

P.j. 'Little Heath' grows to 50 cm (20 in) with small cream-white variegated leaves; new shoots are flushed pink. Sh/E C

All Pieris need acid soil.

PILEOSTEGIA

P. viburnoides grows to 6 m (20 ft) with dark green leathery leaves. Pleasing globular cream flower buds. Self-clinging. Cl/E C

PINUS

P. mugo (mountain pine) grows to 4.5 m (15 ft) with green needles. *P.m.* 'Pumilio' is usually prostrate and seldom achieves 1.8 m (6 ft). T/E C or S

P. pinea (stone pine) grows to 7.5 m (25 ft) with dark green needles and a characteristic low-domed shape. T/E S

P. radiata (Monterey pine) grows to 15 m (50 ft) with bright green needles. Fast-growing. T/E S

PITTOSPORUM

P. tenuifolium grows to 4.5 m (15 ft). Black stems of attractive pale green leaves having wavy edges. Sh/E C or S

P.t. 'Ella Keightley' has pale green leaves with conspicuous yellow blotches. Tender. Sh/E C

P.t. 'Variegatum' has leaves margined with creamy white. Tender. Sh/E C

P.t. 'Garnettii' is more columnar, with grey-green leaves margined white, this turning pink in winter. Sh/E C

P.t. 'Purpureum' has pale green young leaves later turning purple. Sh/E C

P.t. 'Silver Queen' has silver-grey leaves. Sh/E C

POLYGONUM

P. cuspidatum grows to 2.4 m (8 ft) with attractive bright green leaves and red stems. White flowers. A rampant colonizer only to be introduced by the brave into their gardens. Rh Div

POPULUS

P. alba (white poplar) grows to 12 m (40 ft) with grey-green leaves that are white beneath. T/D C or suckers.

P. candicans (syn. *P. gileadensis*) 'Aurora' grows to 7.5 m (25 ft) or more with beautiful young foliage that is creamy white splashed with pink; the leaves later turn to pale green but they are still splashed pink or white. The best way to attain and keep this foliage is to pollard the poplar in early spring. T/D C or suckers.

POTENTILLA

P. anserina (silverweed) grows to 23 cm (9 in) but travels extensively by means of runners. Silver-backed feather-shaped foliage. Yellow flowers. HP R

PRUNUS

P. cerasifera 'Atropurpurea' (syn. 'Pissardii') grows to 7.5 m (25 ft) with shining dark red leaves. Pale pink flowers and, later, small early plums. T/D G

P. laurocerasus (cherry or common laurel) grows to 6 m (20 ft) with shining dark green leaves. Pendulous racemes of cream flowers. Sh/E C or S

P.l. 'Marbled White' is slow-growing with foliage conspicuously marbled grey-green and white. Sh/E C

P.l. 'Otto Luyken' has neat shining dark green leaves. White flowers. Sh/E C

P. lusitanica 'Variegata' has foliage with conspicuous cream margins often turning pink in winter. Sh/E C

PULMONARIA

P. officinalis (lungwort) grows to 30 cm (12 in) with white-spotted hispid green leaves. Pink and blue flowers. HP Div

P. saccharata grows to 30 cm (12 in) with spots and blotches of silver-white. Best in humus-rich, moist soil. HP Div

[Text continues on p. 68

The mounding silver-grey leaves of *Senecio greyi* (*Senecio laxifolius*) are a perfect foil for this young variegated euonymus.

Pebbles make a soft but multicoloured setting for the beautiful foliage of rheum, phormium, and hosta, with the tracery of bamboo behind.

PYRUS
P. salicifolia 'Pendula' (willow-leaved pear) grows to 4.5 m (15 ft) or more with graceful branches of narrow, silvery leaves. T/D   G

QUERCUS
Q. coccinea (scarlet oak) grows to 9 m (30 ft) with pointed lobes to the mid-green leaves. Astonishing autumn colour. *Q.p.* 'Splendens' is even better. T/D   S or G
Q. ilex (Holm oak, evergreen oak) grows to 9 m (30 ft) with dark green leaves having grey undersides. Not always hardy. T/E   S

RAOULIA
R. australis grows only 1 cm (½ in) high with minute silver-blue leaves. Tender. Suc   S or Div

RHEUM
R. palmatum 'Rubra' grows to 2.5 m (8 ft) with large, crimson-toned rhubarb-like green leaves. Protect from slugs. Best in damp soil. Crimson flowers. HP   Div

RHODODENDRON
Very many species and varieties are grown for their beautiful flowers but for the rest of the year they make excellent hedging. For background green, *R. ponticum* grows to 6 m (20 ft) with glossy dark green leaves. Pink-purple flower trusses. Acid soil essential. Sh/E   S/L/G or C

RHUS
R. typhina (stag's horn sumach) grows to 4.5 m (15 ft) with beautiful pinnate green leaves that change to orange, crimson and scarlet in autumn. Invasive. Sh/D   C or suckers

RICINUS
R. communis (castor-oil plant) grows rapidly to 1.5 m (5 ft), with handsome, shiny, palmate leaves in green or bronze. *R.c.* 'Gibsonii' has bronze foliage. *R.c.* 'Sanguineus' has red-purple foliage and *R.c.* 'Zanzibarensis' has huge leaves 25 cm (10 in) across (needs a sheltered site). The seeds of all are very poisonous. HHA   S

ROBINIA
R. pseudoacacia grows to 9 m (30 ft) with delicate, light green leaflets. T/D   S or suckers
R.p. 'Frisia' has distinctive light yellow-green foliage;

it is tender and fragile. T/D   S

RODGERSIA
R. pinnata grows to 1.2 m (4 ft) with very handsome pinnate, deeply veined green or bronze-green leaves. *R.p.* 'Superba' is the finest, with bronze-purple foliage. Beautiful with iris and hosta. Pink flowers. Must have damp soil. Rh   Div or S
R. tabularis grows to 90 cm (3 ft) with scallop-edged parasol leaves often to 90 cm (3 ft) across. Cream flowers. Good in smaller waterside planting where gunnera might be overwhelming. Rh   Div or S

ROSA
R. rubrifolia grows to 2.1 m (7 ft) with distinctive mauve-grey leaves. Small pink flowers and pleasing dark hips. Sh/D   G/C or S

ROSMARINUS
R. lavandulaceus (prostrate rosemary) grows to 10 cm (4 in) with a spread of up to 1.2 m (4 ft). Mid to light green leaves, blue-mauve flowers. Tender. Sh/E   C

RUBUS
R. idaeus 'Aureus' grows to 45 cm (18 in) with season-long bright yellow leaves. Sh/D   L
R. tricolor grows only to 15 cm (6 in) but has 1.8 m (6 ft) runners in a season. Handsome, shining leaves and furred crimson stems. Does well in semi-shade. Invasive and rampant and consequently useful in difficult places. Sh/E   L

RUSCUS
R. aculeatus (butcher's broom) grows to 60 cm (2 ft) with sharply pointed leaves. Dioecious. Minute green flowers and red berries when it feels like it. Very enduring in shade. Sh/E   Div or S

RUTA
R. graveolens 'Jackman's Blue' grows to 60 cm (2 ft) with glaucous blue foliage. Best in semi-shade. Unremarkable yellow flowers. Clip back in spring. Sh/E   C or S

SALIX
S. babylonica (weeping willow) grows to 7.5 m (25 ft) with pendulous branches of pale to mid-green leaves. Good for contrast background colour and shape. T/D   C
S. × *boydii* grows to 30 cm (12 in) with a gnarled, 'bonsai'

appearance. Deeply veined, corrugated grey leaves. Sh/D C

SALVIA

S. argentea grows to 45 cm (18 in) or more with large, silky soft grey-white leaves. White and mauve flowers. Protect in winter. HHP (best as Bi) Off

S. officinalis 'Icterina' (golden sage) grows to a rounded 60 cm (2 ft) with marbled foliage of yellow and green. Tender. Sh/E C

S. purpurescens (purple sage) grows to a lax 60 cm (2 ft) or more with soft plum-purple foliage, occasionally variegated. Blue flowers. Sh/E C

S. 'Tricolor' grows to 60 cm (2 ft) with brightly variegated foliage of white, cerise, purple and green. Needs a hot spot. Tender. Sh/E C

SAMBUCUS

S. racemosa 'Plumosa Aurea' grows to 3 m (10 ft) with finely cut yellow leaves that change to light green if the shrub is planted in semi-shade. In full sun it may get scorched but it stays yellow. Sh/D C

SANTOLINA

S. chamaecyparissus (cotton lavender) grows to 60 cm (2 ft) with woolly, silver-grey leaves. May be kept clipped to mini-hedge shape or allowed to grow naturally. Yellow flowers. Sh/E C

SASA

S. palmata grows to 2.4 m (8 ft) with large green leaves (these wither at the edges in cold winters). Invasive, but good as a background or boundary plant in a sheltered garden. Bam/E Div

SAXIFRAGA

S. stolonifera (mother of thousands) grows to 8 cm (3 in) with almost round dark green hairy leaves veined in white. These are very striking – all the more so because this is generally regarded as a houseplant. In appropriately sheltered corners it is quite hardy. White flowers. *S.s.* 'Tricolor' has leaves edged and variegated in pink and is more delicate – it could not withstand outdoor winter temperatures. THP/E Off

S. × *urbium* (London pride) grows to 5 cm (2 in) with neat, dark green rosettes. Pink flowers. LC/E Div

SEDUM

(Those not marked E die back in the winter.)

S. acre 'Aureum' grows to 5 cm (2 in) with pale-yellow tipped shoots. Yellow flowers. Suc/E Div

S. × 'Autumn Joy' grows to 60 cm (2 ft) with pleasing jade-green succulent leaves. Pink flowers. Suc Div

S. maximum 'Atropurpureum' grows to 90 cm (3 ft) with striking succulent dark crimson foliage and flowers. Tender. Suc Div

S. spathulifolium 'Cappa Blanca' grows to 5 cm (2 in) with succulent blue-white foliage. *S.s.* 'Purpureum' has purple leaves. Suc/E Div

SEMPERVIVUM

Many species, varieties and colours of these sculptural plants are available; they are of differing degrees of hardiness. All need a sunny, well-drained situation. Protect newly planted groups from birds. Suc Off

S. arachnoideum (cobweb houseleek) grows to 2.5 cm (1 in) with 'webbed' leaf-rosettes. Pink-red flowers. Protect from winter wet or take into conservatory.

S. 'Rubin' has red-bronze rosettes. Pink flowers.

S. tectorum (common houseleek) grows to 8 cm (3 in), a group will spread to 30 cm (12 in) or more. Maroon-tipped green leaves. Rose-purple flowers.

S.t. 'Othello' has very large all-crimson rosettes.

SENECIO

S. greyi (syn. *S. laxifolius*) grows to 1.2 m (4 ft) with silver-white shoots, stems and undersides to the leaves which are dark green above. Yellow flowers. Good in exposed and maritime areas. Sh/E C

S. maritima (syn. *Cineraria maritima*) grows to 60 cm (2 ft) with silver-white dissected leaves; remove developing flower stems. 'White Diamond' and 'Silver Dust' are excellent foliage varieties, the latter having fern-like leaves. HHA S

SOPHORA

S. tetraptera (Kowhai) grows to 6 m (20 ft) with sprays of minute green leaflets. Yellow flowers. Tender. T/E S

SORBUS

S. aria (common whitebeam) grows to 6 m (20 ft) with silver-white young foliage, upper sides later becoming green. T/D S

SPARTIUM

S. junceum grows to 3 m (10 ft) with emerald green,

[Text continues on p. 73

The beautifully variegated leaves of griselinia make an arresting feature in any garden.

Silver sea holly is set off perfectly by bergenia, with euphorbias and the young foliage of *Onopordon Acanthium. Stipa gigantea* is seen to perfection against the darkness of the hedge.

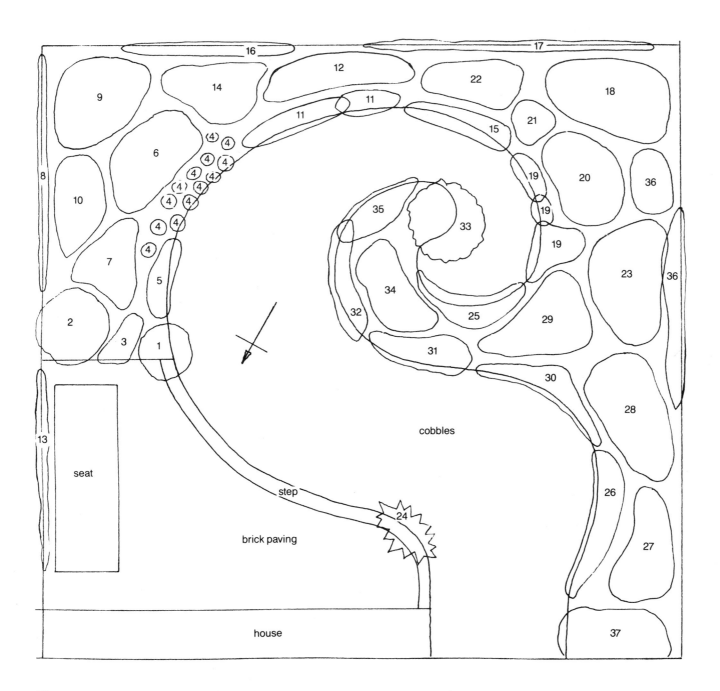

Fig. 8. The Very Small Garden

The 'new development' garden is often very small indeed, this one measures 5½ m × 5½ m (18 ft × 18 ft) and is planted mainly with small-leaved subjects to make the most of every available inch. (See also p. 17.)

1. Salix boydii
2. Ballota pseudodictamnus
3. Alchemilla alpina
4. Sempervivums
5. Euphorbia myrsinites
6. Hebe pinguifolia 'Pagei'
7. Ajuga
8. Hedera 'Goldheart'
9. Spiraea × bumalda 'Goldflame'
10. Artemisia absinthium 'Lambrook Silver'
11. Ophiopogon planiscapus nigrescens
12. Houttuynia cordata or Coleus or Pelargoniums
13. Hedera 'Buttercup'
14. Abies concolor 'Glauca compacta'
15. Vinca minor 'Variegata'
16. Lonicera japonica 'Aureoreticulata'
17. Hedera 'Sagittaefolia'
18. Euonymus 'Silver Queen'
19. Lamium 'Beacon Silver'
20. Berberis thunbergii 'Atropurpurea Nana'
21. Hosta
22. Ruta 'Jackman's Blue'
23. Lonicera 'Baggesen's Gold'
24. Phormium or Palm
25. Acaena
26. Pachysandra
27. Cheiranthus 'Bowles' Mauve'
28. Helichrysum angustifolium
29. Arundinaria viridistriata
30. Mitella breweri
31. Saxifraga × urbium
32. Lysimachia nummularia 'Aurea'
33. Taxus baccata 'Standishii' or clipped topiary
34. Corokia cotoneaster
35. Cerastium tomentosum 'Columnae'
36. Euonymus 'Emerald 'n Gold'
37. Fuchsia magellanica 'Gracilis'

almost leafless branches. Yellow flowers. A good 'contrast' plant for texture, shape and colour. Sh/E   S

SPIRAEA

S. × bumalda 'Goldflame' grows to 80 cm (2½ ft) with yellow and crimson spring growth which eventually fades to light green. Pink flowers. Sh/D   C

STACHYS

S. lanata (lamb's ears) grows to 45 cm (18 in) with soft, silver-furred leaves. Pale mauve flowers. *S.l.* 'Silver Carpet' is flowerless but more tender. HP/E   Div

TAMARIX

T. pentandra (tamarisk) grows to 4.5 m (15 ft) with airy branches of light green leaves, good as a contrast plant. Pink flowers. Sh/E   C

TANACETUM

T. densum 'Amani' syn. *T. haradjanii* grows to 20 cm (8 in) with silver feather-shaped leaves. Must have sharp drainage and sun. HP/E   Div

TAXODIUM

T. distichum (swamp cypress) grows to 10.5 m (35 ft) or more with exquisite pale green dissected foliage that turns to russet in autumn. T/D   S

TAXUS

T. baccata (yew) grows to 4.5 m (15 ft) with dark green foliage. Excellent as hedging and backgrounds. It has several coloured varieties. T/E   C or S

T.b. 'Aurea' has golden green leaves, gradually changing to green. T/E   C

T.b. 'Fastigiata' (Irish yew) has black-green leaves and was usually planted in churchyards. T/E   C

T.b. 'Standishii' is slow-growing and is columnar, with golden yellow leaves. T/E   C

TELLIMA

T. grandiflora grows to 60 cm (2 ft) with attractive semi-circular green leaves. Greenish-bronze flowers. *T.g.* 'Purpurea' has purplish leaves in winter and early spring. Good in semi-shade. HP/E   Div or S

THUJA

T. occidentalis 'Rheingold' grows only to 90 cm (3 ft) with a spread of 60 cm (2 ft). Golden foliage, best in winter. T/E   C

THYMUS

T. × citriodorus 'Aureus' (golden thyme) has fragrant golden foliage. Needs sun. Tender. Sh/E   C

TOLMIEA

T. menziesii (pick-a-back plant) grows to 20 cm with rounded green leaves, many having plantlets growing on them for forming new plants. HP/E   Plantlet

TRACHYCARPUS

T. fortunei (syn. *Chamaerops excelsa*) (Chusan or fan palm) grows to 3 m (10 ft) with indestructible fan-shaped leaves 90 cm (3 ft) wide. Tender, not for colder areas. Palm/E   S or suckers.

TRADESCANTIA

T. albiflora (wandering Jew) grows or trails to 30 cm

[Text continues on p. 76

The golden foliage of cornus will bring sunshine to this corner whatever the weather.

Blue-leaved hostas, delicate plum-coloured acer foliage and the lightness of the grass, enhance path, brick wall and wood, providing a satisfying variation of textures and colour.

(12 in) or more with green and white striped leaves. Set out in pot for summer. THP/E   C

TRIFOLIUM

T. repens 'Purpurescens Quadriphyllum' grows to 10 cm (4 in) with purple leaflets. Needs sun and well-drained soil. Rh/D   Div

TULIPA

T. greigii 'Red Riding Hood' has purple-streaked green leaves. Red flowers. Bulb   S or Off

VERBASCUM

V. olympicum grows to 2.7 m (9 ft) with white-flannel leaves and stems. Yellow flowers. Bi   S

V. thapsus grows to 1.5 m (5ft) with soft silver-grey leaves (best in first year). Yellow flowers. Bi   S

VIBURNUM

V. davidii grows to 90 cm (3 ft) but spreads wider to 1.5 m (5 ft) Handsome dark green, ovate, deeply veined leaves. White flowers. Dioecious. Blue berries if both sexes are planted together. Sh/E   C or S

V. rhytidophyllum grows to a lanky 4.5 m (15 ft) with handsome, deeply veined leaves. White flowers. Also dioecious. This one has red berries turning to black. Sh/E   C

V. tinus (laurustinus) grows to 3 m (10 ft) and spreads to 2.1 m (7 ft). White flowers. *V.t.* 'Variegatum' has golden variegated leaves. Sh/E   C

VINCA

V. major (greater periwinkle) grows to 30 cm (12 in) with grass-green leaves on far-reaching runners which root at the tips. Vigorous and invasive but good in dry shade. Blue-mauve flowers. Sh/E   Div or R

V.m. 'Elegantissima' grows to 30 cm (12 in) but is not as vigorous. Variegated green and cream leaves, paler blue flowers. Best in sun. Sh/E   Div

V. minor (lesser periwinkle) grows to 10 cm (4 in) with long runners that root at the nodes. Good in shade. Purple flowers. Sh/E   Div or R

V. minor 'Variegata' grows to 8 cm (3 in) and spreads

more gently and very prettily. Blue flowers. Sh/E   Div or R

VITIS

V. coignetiae (glory vine) grows to 27 m (90 ft) with large deeply veined green leaves turning to wonderful autumn scarlet. Cl/D   L

V. vinifera (grape vine) grows to 6 m (20 ft) with vine-shaped green leaves and grapes of various colours according to variety. *V.v.* 'Brandt' colours to crimson, pink and orange in autumn with purple grapes. *V.v.* 'Purpurea' has red to purple foliage throughout the year (more purple in autumn), followed by inedible blue-black grapes. Cl/D   C

WEIGELA

W. florida 'Foliis Purpureis' grows slowly to 1.8 m (6 ft). Pink flowers. 'Variegata' has cream-margined green leaves. 'Looymansii Aurea' has red-margined yellow leaves, best in semi-shade. Sh/D   C

YUCCA

Y. filamentosa grows to 75 cm (2½ ft) with glaucous mid-green leaves. Cream flowers. Sh/E   suckers

Y. gloriosa (Adam's needle) grows to 1.8 m (6 ft) with a similar spread, and deadly spine-tipped darker green leaves. Cream white flowers. Sh/E   suckers

Y. recurvifolia grows to 1.8 m (6 ft) with narrower arching green leaves. Cream-white flowers. Sh/E   suckers

ZANTEDESCHIA (formerly *Richardia aethiopica*)

Z.aethiopica (arum lily) grows to 90 cm (3 ft) with handsome, large arrow-shaped leaves. Cream-white scrolled flowers. Tender. May be kept in large pots in a warm greenhouse (it is not then deciduous) and planted out in pots in summer, or sunk in a pond. Feed well. 'Crowborough' is hardiest. HHRh   Div

ZEA

Z. mays 'Gracillima Variegata' grows to 90 cm (3 ft), with white-striped green leaves. *Z.m.* 'Quadricolor' is bigger and taller, to 1.8 m (6 ft), with pink, white and pale yellow leaves. HHA   S

8

JUST A TOUCH OF COLOUR

This chapter is for those gardeners who are not quite satisfied with the tonal subtleties of all the various greens – in other words, it is for gardeners who want a good jolt of primary colour right in a place where they can see it. Many of these vibrant-coloured plants are of tender tropical origin, so I have included a few notes about their care and propagation.

First, there is absolutely nothing to beat the wonderful *Coleus blumei* family, whose unbelievable colours are often brighter (and certainly less subtle) than many a border flower. They cannot, of course, be set out – either in tubs, troughs or pots – until the warm weather is constant, but they can be chosen, sown, grown on and carefully hardened off, in preparation. They should then be sited in a semi-shaded position because strong sunlight will scorch or fade the amazing colours of the leaves.

There are packets of mixed seeds which can be a bran-tubful of jolly surprises, or specific colours which are named and sold separately. The plants need to be properly grown on, and a warm greenhouse is best for this. The seeds should be surface-sown in midwinter at a constant temperature of 18–20°C (65–75°F). Germination should take place within twenty days. When large enough, transplant into John Innes No. 1 and grow on, potting on as needed, turning the plants round daily to the light if necessary. Seeds are obtainable in shades such as 'Red Monarch', 38–45 cm (15–18 in) which is all-red variety; 'Salmon Laced', 45 cm (18 in), which has a bright central area of salmon pink to cerise, surrounded by a 'lace edging' of green, cream, yellow, white and black. 'Scarlet Poncho', to 30 cm (12 in), has more flexible branches and is very suitable to drip colourfully over the edge of troughs, pots and hanging baskets. It is crimson to maroon with a neat narrow yellow edge. Most of the other varieties are sold as 'mixed', and very beautiful they are, because in addition to the almost unreal colours, there is a new range of leaf-shapes such as oak-leaved, sabre-leaved, and some smaller types whose foliage resembles an underwater coral reef. These plants can make a midsummer flower border in full glory look positively pallid.

Favourite plants can be vegetatively propagated by means of non-flowering cuttings 8 cm (3 in) long taken in late summer or early spring. Place these round the rim of a pot of John Innes No. 1 and put into a propagator set at 16–18°C (61–64°F). When rooted, they can be transferred into individual pots of John Innes No. 1 and grown on. Always pinch out any flowers as soon as these are seen forming and bring the outdoor plants in as soon as the nights start to cool.

There is a bright-leaved pelargonium called 'Mrs Henry Cox' whose gay foliage includes shades of green, black, yellow, red and pink. Another called 'Dolly Varden' is similar but rather more muted.

The annual *Amaranthus tricolor* 'Joseph's Coat' lives up to its name, with brilliant red and yellow foliage. It needs full sun to give of its best.

Many 'greenhouse' begonias are quite happy in a sheltered garden for the summer, and of these, the Rex varieties are outstanding with silver edges, patterns or zones on dark green, red or purple leaves, highlighted with pink, lilac, cream or light lime green. These are propagated from seed or from leaf cuttings. For the latter, take a good newly matured leaf and its stem and lay this on a pan of damp rooting compost (equal quantities of peat and sand). Make cuts into the main veins on the underside of the leaf, and hold down in position with clean pebbles. Put the pan into a propagator set at 18–21°C (64–70°F) until plantlets develop; keep moist. When these have produced leaves, separate the new plant from the 'parent' leaf and pot up in John Innes No. 1. I have had Rex begonias out of doors in my garden for a (warm) summer season with great success; they need a sheltered, shaded position and regular fortnightly feeding, and as all begonias have fragile stems they need discreet support to prevent damage from high winds. Feed regularly and bring back into the greenhouse for the winter as soon as the night temperature drops below 13°C (55°F).

Houttuynia cordata 'Variegata' is another brilliantly-coloured foliage plant which is said to be quite hardy so I am trying it out in my garden. It is most successful with the summer foliage of Kochia, the striped green and white leaves of *Phalaris arundinacea* 'Picta' 'Gardener's Garters' and a sprawl of the golden pennies of *Lysimachia nummularia* 'Aurea' (creeping Jenny) in front to echo the yellow in the leaves of the Houttuynia.

Prunus laurocerasus

INDEX